DAIRY-FREE
Delicious

DAIRY-FREE
Delicious

KATY SALTER

PHOTOGRAPHY BY LAURA EDWARDS

Quadrille
PUBLISHING

For Mum and Dad, for everything.

PUBLISHING DIRECTOR: Jane O'Shea
CREATIVE DIRECTOR: Helen Lewis
SENIOR EDITOR: Céline Hughes
DESIGN: Katherine Keeble
PHOTOGRAPHY: Laura Edwards
FOOD STYLIST: Emily Jonzen
PROPS STYLIST: Tabitha Hawkins
PRODUCTION: Vincent Smith, Sasha Hawkes

First published in 2015 by
Quadrille Publishing Limited
Pentagon House
52-54 Southwark Street
London SE1 1UN

www.quadrille.co.uk

Cataloguing in Publication Data: a catalogue record for this book is
available from the British Library.

ISBN: 978 1 84949 490 8

Printed in China

INTRODUCTION

MY STORY

Lactose intolerance was not in the plan. My three great loves as a child were reading, writing and eating. As an adult, I have been lucky enough to combine the latter two and make a living out of them. I became a journalist and eventually landed my dream job as features editor of a food magazine.

The unofficial job description of a food writer is to 'go everywhere; eat everything', and for several years I did just that - trying everything from Croatian truffle ice cream to Kenyan crocodile. The ability to eat weird and wonderful foods was something I took for granted.

Then food poisoning struck. A few bouts of gastroenteritis followed. My once Teflon stomach was now weak, and I would often be sick for no obvious reason. Unexplained and extremely painful stomach cramps meant I was regularly off sick from work, and, when I wasn't, I felt permanently exhausted. It seems obvious in retrospect, but at the time I didn't make the connection to my diet. I spent half of 2011 at the doctors having blood tests for various conditions - everything (blessedly) came back negative.

Eventually, I was told to try two elimination diets and keep a food diary. The first two weeks were spent cutting out gluten, which made no difference - the cramps and nausea were as bad as ever. The second test was a dairy elimination diet - no butter, no yogurt, no cheese and certainly no milk. The changes were instant and profound. No more stomach cramps, no more nausea, and my energy started to return - no more feeling like a pensioner shuffling round pretending to be a 30-year-old. The dairy had to go. Sure, I missed flat whites, Parmesan and chocolate buttons (especially the chocolate buttons), but I was so happy not to be in pain that it didn't seem like a sacrifice.

The biggest difficulty has been the incompatibility of living dairy free and eating out. After all, this was not just about my diet, food is also my livelihood. Things I took for granted were now tricky - grabbing a pizza with friends, reviewing a French restaurant (all that butter), going to weddings. I reluctantly became that fussy eater who asks for the dressing on the side. It made me realise how intolerant our food culture is of people with dietary requirements - be it people with intolerances, allergies, coeliac disease, vegetarians, vegans, or those who don't eat certain foods for health or religious reasons. Just because you can't eat everything, it doesn't mean you don't love good food. Everyone should feel comfortable and welcome when they eat out.

Sure, there have been times when I've fallen off the wagon a little... and felt the consequences. I lived in New York for part of 2012 and discovered the 'miracle cure' of lactase tablets from the drug store - little supplements that help your body break down lactose. They helped for a while but after doubling up in pain on the pavement after eating a cheeseburger, I realised that living dairy free was permanent for me, something that couldn't be solved by popping a pill. I chose not just to accept it but embrace it, and started creating dairy-free recipes to help people in the same position.

There is no cheeseburger so delicious it's worth crying over. Especially not when, with a few tweaks to your diet, you can live dairy free and enjoy food every bit as delicious as the pizzas, ice creams, chocolates and cheeses you used to eat. There are so many people out there who have problems digesting dairy. Many are people who live to eat, to cook and to entertain just as much as I do. If you're one of them, I hope you find plenty of recipes in this book to reignite your love affair with good food.

WHAT IS LACTOSE INTOLERANCE?

Lactose is a type of sugar found in milk. It can't be absorbed by the body as it is, so when you eat anything containing lactose, the lactase in your digestive system gets to work breaking down the lactose into other simple sugars that can be absorbed into your body. Lactase is an enzyme produced by the body to break down lactose.

The problem is lots of us don't have enough lactase in our systems to break down lactose efficiently. This is where the sexy symptoms start – bloating, stomach cramps and pains, diarrhoea, flatulence and nausea. None of them are life-threatening, but they can seriously impact your quality of life.

Lactose intolerance is exceedingly common. The figures vary, but studies suggest that, for example, 15% of the British population is lactose intolerant. That's 9.5 million people. Worldwide, it's estimated that some 65% of adults have some level of difficulty digesting lactose.

Lactose intolerance is particularly prevalent in certain ethnic groups, including people of East Asian, West African, Jewish and Arabic descent. It's believed that primary lactase deficiency, which is inherited, is particularly common in ethnic groups that have a shorter history of including milk as a key part of their diet.

Lactose intolerance can also occur at any stage in life. This is called secondary lactase deficiency. Babies and young children can be sensitive to dairy but often grow out of it. Both adults and children can develop lactose intolerance after gastroenteritis, after long courses of antibiotics, as a result of chemotherapy, or as a symptom of other conditions including coeliac and Crohn's disease. For some people, secondary lactase deficiency may be temporary. But for others it can be permanent. Either way, our bodies naturally produce less lactase as we age, so adjusting to a diet with less or no dairy in it can be helpful to many.

The severity of lactose intolerance varies from person to person. I can't handle any cow's milk products, including milk chocolate, without getting stomach cramps. But I do eat a little sheep's yogurt and goat's and sheep's cheese in small quantities. Cow's milk typically contains more lactose than that from other dairy animals like goats, sheep and buffalo. I also sometimes drink lactose-free milk, where all the lactose is removed by a special process. The NHS says that 'the exact changes you need to make in your diet depend on how sensitive you are to lactose'. It suggests that if you decide to experiment with which foods you can and can't tolerate, do so gradually.

If you think you might be lactose intolerant, it is always advisable to speak to your doctor first and keep a food and symptoms diary. They may suggest an elimination diet or, in some instances, further blood sugar or other tests that can diagnose lactose intolerance.

WHAT IS A MILK ALLERGY?

Cow's milk allergy is an immune-system response to one or more of the proteins in cow's milk (most commonly casein). This type of allergy is called an IgE-mediated milk allergy. When people with the allergy consume milk, the body goes into red alert, mistakenly producing antibodies to fight off what it perceives as a threat. The symptoms come on quickly and can include a rash or hives, eczema, wheezing and coughing, swollen lips, vomiting and stomach pain. In rare cases, it can cause anaphylaxis, which needs immediate emergency treatment.

There is also another type of cow's milk allergy, called a non-IgE-mediated cow's milk protein allergy. It was formerly called a milk protein intolerance, but the NHS classifies it as an allergy. It is more common in children, and symptoms include eczema, vomiting, stomach cramps and diarrhoea, but not hives or wheezing/breathing problems. The symptoms can take longer to develop than with an IgE-mediated allergy, and can often develop a few hours after consuming milk products.

Milk allergies are more common in children than adults. They affect around 2–5% of babies and young children and usually start in infancy. Luckily, many children with a milk allergy grow out of it and only 0.1% of people over the age of 5 have one.

If you suspect that you or your child has a milk allergy, you should always consult your doctor.

LEARNING TO READ THE LABELS
It's easy to cut milk and cheese out of your diet, but what about all those products that contain milk? Dairy shows up in an astonishing array of foodstuffs, from some breads and crisps to salad dressings and even some wines (I like to think this last one explains some terrible 'miscarriage of justice' hangovers I've had after two glasses of Sauvignon). Always check the label and look out for terms like the following:
* Buttermilk
* Casein
* Caseinates
* Ghee
* Milk protein
* Milk powder
* Milk solids
* Skimmed milk powder
* Whey

THE IMPLICATIONS OF CUTTING OUT DAIRY
If you're cutting out dairy, then it's important to ensure you're getting all the nutrients you would from milk, cheese and yogurt elsewhere in your diet.

Dairy products are a good source of calcium, important for building strong teeth and bones when you're young, and keeping them strong in later life and preventing osteoporosis, as well as for regulating your muscles and heartbeat.

Look for dairy-free milks such as soya, almond and oat milk, which have been fortified with calcium. If you are lactose intolerant, rather than allergic to milk, you could also try lactose-free milk, which uses a special process to remove all the lactose from milk. For babies with a milk allergy, consult your doctor who can advise on the most suitable type of formula.

There are many other good dietary sources of calcium and you will find many recipes using them in this book. Include the following in your diet wherever possible:
* Dark leafy greens like kale, broccoli and watercress
* Most nuts, including almonds, Brazil nuts and hazelnuts
* Tofu
* Pulses
* Sesame seeds
* Salmon
* Sardines
* Soya beans
* Wholegrains, including wholegrain bread

Adults need 700mg of calcium a day, preferably from your diet, and a balanced dairy-free diet that includes non-dairy milks and the foods above should do this. If you're concerned about the amount of calcium in your diet, talk to your doctor before taking supplements, as supplements in high doses can be harmful.

Our bodies also need Vitamin D to absorb calcium. We get most of this from sunlight, but if you live in a rainy land like Britain, it's also a good idea to include the following in your diet, which are all good sources of Vitamin D:
* Eggs
* Fortified cereals
* Oily fish

SO WHAT CAN YOU EAT INSTEAD OF DAIRY?
The good news is, there are lots of delicious dairy alternatives you can eat – and the situation is improving all the time. My local café now does an almond-milk flat white and some supermarkets now stock coconut yogurt. Both were unthinkable even a few years ago.

One important thing to note is that you don't need to panic-buy lots of processed, expensive free-from products that are stuffed with weird, unpronounceable ingredients. There are lots of free-from biscuits, cakes and snacks on the market but I hope this book shows that it's really easy to make your own. In many cases it will be cheaper, and it will give you more control over what you and your family are eating. I've tried to stick to natural ingredients in this book wherever possible, and certainly to avoid anything with glucose-fructose/high-fructose corn syrup in it.

Nut, rice, coconut, oat and soya milk are now available in corner shops and supermarkets, and will form a key part of your dairy-free diet. Look for ones from non-GM and sustainable sources where appropriate. It's also easy to make your own nut, oat and rice milks, which have the added benefit of being free from any emulsifiers and stabilisers. There are recipes for all of these on pages 40-41 in the breakfast chapter, and a recipe for Mexican-style horchata in the dessert chapter (see page 154). A cool glass of horchata on a hot day is every bit as irresistible as a glass of milk.

There is still lingering confusion over eggs and whether or not they are dairy. Eggs are not dairy. Assuming you are not vegan or allergic to eggs, then enjoy at your will – I use them in many recipes in this book (free-range, naturally).

Meat, fish, pulses, nuts and all fruits and vegetables are all naturally dairy free. So are animal fats such as duck and goose fat (for delicious roasties or the duck confit on page 75) and lard (which makes delicious savoury pastry). Oils such as olive and rapeseed can often be used instead of butter in cooking, and in cakes (for more on this see pages 12-13).

For a full list of useful ingredients to include in your diet, turn to the store cupboard section on pages 10-13.

HOW THIS BOOK WORKS
All the recipes in this book are 100% dairy free. The book is specifically aimed at people who can't or won't eat dairy, rather than a generalist free-from book, but I have tried to include a decent number of options for those with other dietary restrictions. Equally, most of the recipes using almond milk can be made with soya milk and vice versa if you cannot eat one or the other.

The recipes in this book can broadly be divided into two types…

The first are those recipes based on dishes or ingredients from countries where dairy forms a very minimal part of the diet. Good examples of these include the creamy Vietnamese curry on page 82 or the Khao soi noodles inspired by a Thai street food dish on page 66. As a side note, when eating out I find Vietnamese, Thai or Japanese restaurants among the best bets for dairy-free dining. French and Italian are probably the trickiest.

The second type of recipes are those that would normally be made with dairy. No one should have to live without pizza, ice cream, chocolate birthday cake or lasagne, so I have devised dairy-free alternatives. Most of the classic dairy dishes are here – from eggs Benedict with a silky hollandaise (see page 22) to a Victoria sandwich filled with vanilla whipped coconut cream (see page 147). There's no fondue, but I think we'll just have to learn to live without cauldrons of melted cheese. Otherwise, with a little determination and adjustment (some dairy-free alternatives don't behave quite as milk or cream would), I believe most dishes can be made *Dairy-Free Delicious*.

A FEW NOTES ON THE RECIPES
* All eggs are large unless otherwise stated
* All lemons are unwaxed
* All almond and soya milk is unsweetened
* All coconut milk is the full-fat kind
* All mayonnaise is the full-fat kind
* Always check the label as some free-from products contain glucose-fructose/high-fructose corn syrup - I have tried to avoid using such products in all the book's recipes

THE DAIRY-FREE STORE CUPBOARD

Stock your fridge and larder with these versatile ingredients and you'll always be ready to make a wealth of delicious dairy-free meals and desserts.

ALMONDS

Almonds are a rich source of calcium, so sprinkle flaked ones on your cereal or Bircher muesli in the mornings, and keep a bag of whole almonds on hand to snack on at work. I use toasted flaked almonds in baking and breakfast recipes, and as an alternative to Parmesan to top salads such as the classic Caesar on page 46.

ALMOND MILK

An incredibly useful and versatile dairy-free ingredient. Not only does unsweetened almond milk contain calcium and taste pleasant in tea and on cereal, its subtle, neutral flavour means it works well as a baking ingredient and substitute for cow's milk. You can also mix almond milk with a little lemon juice as an alternative to buttermilk. Look for brands made with non-GM ingredients, fortified with vitamins like B12 and E, and always without sugar (all the recipes using almond milk in this book are made with unsweetened almond milk). Commercial nut milks are emulsified so can sometimes separate when added straight to the pan during cooking, so for savoury dishes, such as the Dauphinoise potatoes on page 77, you can make a basic white sauce to avoid this happening.

AVOCADOS

Avocados are sometimes known as 'butter pears', which is a perfect description of the creamy flesh hidden inside that scaly, fat-bottomed exterior. Avocados are packed with nutrients like Vitamin E, iron and potassium and are a useful dairy-free ingredient – use them to make chocolate mousse or spread on toast for breakfast.

BAKING MARGARINE

Use block baking margarine to make flaky pastry, airy sponge cakes and short biscuits. It may not match the delights of real butter when it comes to taste, but it's a good substitute for unsalted butter in baking as it has a similar consistency. Depending on the recipe, I often use a little vanilla extract or cinnamon to enhance the flavour of the cake or biscuit and make up for the lack of that creamy, real-butter taste. People can never tell the difference! Look for brands made with sustainable palm oil and without trans fats, such as Stork. Be careful to avoid the spreadable kinds, however, as they contain buttermilk.

CACAO NIBS

Cacao nibs are little roasted chips of the cacao bean. They are usually ground into a paste to make chocolate, but are increasingly popular as a food in their own right (find them in health food stores). The first time you try cacao nibs can be disconcerting, especially if you're used to sweet milk chocolate. They have an intense, earthy flavour - chocolatey but not sweet. After you've got used to them, they're very moreish - which is good news as cacao is packed with antioxidants and minerals, including magnesium. Eat a handful as a snack, sprinkle onto cereal and porridge or use in the cacao nib and cranberry granola or raw chocolate and espresso granita recipes (see pages 28 and 122 respectively).

CASHEW NUTS

Creamy, biscuity cashews have a multitude of uses in a dairy-free diet. Make delicious cashew milk to drink or pour over cereal, spread cashew butter on toast, make cashew cream to serve with desserts (the recipe for macadamia cream on page 34 can also be made with the same weight of cashews), or use instead of cheese in savoury dishes like curries, stir-fries and pesto. Not only do cashews taste delicious, they're also a great source of magnesium and zinc.

COCOA POWDER

A dairy-free diet doesn't mean you have to give up your favourite chocolate desserts. Good quality 70% cocoa doesn't contain cow's milk so you can use it in cakes and puds, and to make hot chocolate. If you're lactose-intolerant then most brands should be okay to use (I like Green & Blacks) - they don't contain any milk in the product but will have a warning on the label saying they 'may contain milk traces' because they're produced in factories that may also produce milk chocolates. If you have a dairy allergy or want to make certain there are no traces, look for dairy-free or vegan brands that are guaranteed free from traces of milk.

COCONUT CREAM

Thick, luscious coconut cream is the best substitute for double or clotted cream. It has a mild flavour that goes well with vanilla and, if you chill it in the fridge first, it whisks up into fluffy clouds of whipped coconut cream. All brands are not created equal, so find one with a pleasant taste that thickens up well when chilled. I like Blue Dragon, in the UK.

COCONUT MILK

People sometimes tell me they 'hate' coconut, but this mild and creamy milk doesn't have the overpowering taste of desiccated coconut or Bounty bars - it's subtle and incredibly useful in dairy-free cooking, so I urge you to give it a try. Coconut milk forms the base of incredible ice creams, a wealth of classic curries and noodle dishes from India and south-east Asia, and it's pretty much one of the most versatile ingredients you can keep in your cupboard. Please note all the recipes using coconut milk in this book are made with full-fat coconut milk - dishes like the ice cream and custard just won't work with the watery, reduced-fat stuff. Try a few brands until you find one you like - again, I like Blue Dragon which always has a delicious thick layer of coconut cream at the top of the can, much like gold-top milk.

COCONUT OIL

Yes, more coconut! Heart-healthy coconut oil comes from the meaty coconut flesh and is solid at room temperature but melts with a little gentle heating. Look for extra-virgin raw coconut oil and use it to make homemade granola or flapjacks, or for frying and roasting vegetables such as the caramelised Chantenay carrots on page 105.

COCONUT YOGURT

Warning: coconut yogurt is addictive. Luckily it's good for you – a vegan yogurt with probiotic cultures made from coconut milk. It has a creamy taste with a slightly sour tang – similar to Greek yogurt, and a voluptuous, thick consistency. Find it in some larger supermarkets or health food stores.

DAIRY-FREE SUNFLOWER SPREAD

I won't lie to you – there's no free-from spread that can compare to the taste of salted butter on a crusty baguette. But for cooking and baking, dairy-free sunflower spread is incredibly versatile. I like Pure dairy-free spread, which is spreadable straight from the fridge, but whichever brand you go for, check it's free from trans fats. Always read the label because some sunflower spreads contain buttermilk.

DARK CHOCOLATE

70%-cocoa-solids dark chocolate is a key ingredient in many of the cakes and desserts in this book. Always check the label – good-quality brands don't contain any milk products, but some cheaper or flavoured ones can. As with the cocoa powder, dark chocolate sometimes comes with a 'may contain milk traces' warning depending on the factory where it was made, so if you have a dairy allergy, look for specialist dairy-free brands.

DARK LEAFY GREENS

Green leafy vegetables like kale, watercress and broccoli are an excellent source of calcium, among many other nutrients, so make a daily Get-your-greens juice in the morning (see page 16), or add these veggies to dishes whenever you can.

MAYONNAISE

I've been asked lots of times if mayonnaise contains dairy. The short answer is – it shouldn't. Good-quality, full-fat mayonnaise like Hellmann's is made with eggs and oil, like mayonnaise should be. It's the reduced-fat brands that often add milk products, so always check the label or, if in doubt, make your own.

MUSTARD POWDER

Mustard powder is what I call a 'disguiser'. I use a little to mask the taste of oat cream or sunflower spread in a savoury sauce and to ape the savoury bite of mature Cheddar or Parmesan. You'll find spices like nutmeg and cinnamon, and lots of vanilla used in the sweet recipes in this book for the same reason. Keeping a well-stocked spice drawer pays dividends for the dairy-free cook.

OAT CREAM

Oat cream is made by emulsifying oats with oil. In terms of colour and consistency, it is a good alternative to single cream in baking. I don't tend to pour it on desserts because there's no getting around the earthy taste (make cashew or macadamia cream, or a batch of whipped coconut cream for this purpose instead). It does have a tendency to split when heated, so for many savoury recipes I find it works better when added to a béchamel or simple white sauce instead, with a little mustard powder (see above).

OLIVE OIL

Light olive oil makes incredible cakes – fluffy sponges and moist chocolate numbers. It's not a straightforward case of swapping the same volume of oil for weight of butter, so stick to the volume specified in the recipes.

PANKO

Panko are crispy and very dry Japanese breadcrumbs. They add colour, crunch and texture to the top of savoury dishes like lasagne, which would normally be topped with cheese.

RICE MILK

Rice milk is one of the most pleasant dairy-free milks to drink on its own, especially ones flavoured with vanilla. It's also easy to make your own (see page 40). However, I don't tend to use it much in cooking as it is quite thin and watery compared to the more robust almond or soya milks. It's also important to note that the NHS in the UK does not recommend rice milk for children under 5 years because it contains low levels of inorganic arsenic.

SESAME SEEDS

Another excellent source of calcium, so get sprinkling sesame seeds on yogurt, salads, curries and a million other dishes.

SOYA MILK AND YOGURT

There are lots of conflicting studies on the health benefits, or otherwise, of soya milk. For those who can't eat nuts as well as dairy it can be a very useful alternative, so I have included it in this book, albeit sparingly as I'm not a huge fan of the taste. Look for brands fortified with calcium. All the recipes using soya milk in this book use the unsweetened version. Many of the recipes using almond milk can also be made using soya if you prefer.

TOFU

Tofu is a good source of calcium. It also takes on strong flavours easily, so it's a brilliant addition to curries, Thai and Vietnamese dishes.

VANILLA

You'll find I've used vanilla extract in many of the book's sweet recipes, as its comforting aroma subtly masks free-from products such as sunflower spread. Use a good-quality real vanilla extract (rather than the cheaper vanillin). I'm also a big fan of real vanilla powder – a tiny pinch is a quick alternative to scraping the seeds from a vanilla pod.

VEGAN CREAM CHEESE

Vegan cream cheese is usually made from tofu. I wouldn't eat it plain or smear it on a bagel as it has – shall we say – an acquired taste, but it whips up with icing sugar and lemon or vanilla into a delicious, fluffy frosting for cakes.

VEGETABLE, GROUNDNUT, RAPESEED OR SUNFLOWER OIL

These neutral cooking oils are used throughout the book, and not just for savoury dishes – they also make light and delicious cakes.

VEGETABLE SHORTENING

Vegetable shortening is a solid fat that makes perfect crumbly pastry. Look for brands that don't contain trans fats and that use palm oil from sustainable sources.

BREAKFAST

ICED MOCHA

1 tablespoon cocoa powder
1 ½ tablespoons maple syrup
1 teaspoon vanilla extract
1 shot of freshly-brewed espresso
250ml vanilla soya or rice milk,
    chilled
Ice cubes

Serves 1

Wish you could drink those coffee shop mochas that come laced with milk and chocolate syrup? Make your own at home with your favourite dairy-free milk and a jolt of espresso to kick-start the morning.

Put the cocoa powder, maple syrup and vanilla in a mixing jug. Pour in the hot espresso and whisk to combine. Leave to cool.

Once cool, pour in the soya or rice milk and whisk again. Add a few ice cubes to a highball glass. Pour over the mocha mixture and drink.

GET-YOUR-GREENS JUICE

50g baby leaf spinach
25g watercress
100g cucumber, cut into chunks
2 eating apples, cored and cut
    into chunks
Large handful of mint
Juice of ½ lime

Serves 1

Delicious, nutritious leafy vegetables: we all know we should be eating more of them. Green juice is an easy way to sneak some breakfast veg into your diet, and here's my take. Packed with spinach, watercress and cucumber, with added apple for sweetness (because no one wants to down a pint of pure watercress).

Add all the ingredients to your juicer according to the instructions. Stir the juice once and pour into a glass. Feel virtuous.

BANANA AND RASPBERRY SHAKE

1 very ripe banana, frozen whole
    in its skin
75g raspberries
25g porridge oats
½ teaspoon ground nutmeg
2 teaspoons honey
150ml almond or vanilla
    rice milk

Serves 1

Bruised and blackened bananas never get thrown away in our house. They go into the freezer, whole, waiting to do service in banana breads, muffins and in quick and filling breakfast shakes like this one. Using a frozen banana keeps smoothies and shakes cold and gives them a lovely thick texture that isn't watered down by ice.

Take the banana out of the freezer half an hour before you want to use it. Alternatively, defrost it in the microwave for 10-20 seconds. The idea is to soften it just enough so you can peel the skin off.

Put the peeled banana, raspberries and oats into a blender. Add the nutmeg, honey and almond or rice milk and blitz for 20 seconds, until smooth. Pour into a tall glass, add a straw and drink immediately.

CLASSIC PANCAKES

130g plain flour
Pinch of sea salt
2 medium eggs
350ml almond, soya or rice milk
Vegetable oil, for frying

Makes 8-10

Thin pancakes, or crêpes, can easily be made dairy-free, using your favourite dairy-free milk (I normally use almond). Top with classic lemon and sugar, sliced banana and maple syrup, summer berries and whipped coconut cream (see page 137), or apple compote, toasted pecans and a dollop of coconut yogurt.

Sift the flour into a large, lipped bowl and add the salt. Whisk together the eggs and almond, soya or rice milk in a separate jug or bowl. Make a well in the centre of the flour and pour in the egg mixture. Whisk together briskly until you have a smooth batter. Leave to stand for 10 minutes.

Preheat the oven to its lowest setting and place a plate in the middle of the oven.

Heat a small non-stick frying pan over a medium-high heat. Add a few drops of oil, then use a piece of kitchen paper to spread this all over the bottom of the pan until you have a light mist of oil covering the surface (you might want to briefly remove the pan from the heat to do this). Turn the heat up to high.

Pour in around 2 tablespoons of batter (just enough to cover the bottom of the pan). Swirl the batter around until you've covered the bottom of the pan and there's no liquid batter left. Once the edges of the pancake start to come away from the pan, use a wide spatula or fish slice to loosen the pancake and flip it over. Cook for another 20–30 seconds, until both sides are golden and lacy.

Place each pancake on the warmed plate as soon as it is cooked and return to the warmed oven, layering a piece of kitchen paper between each pancake to stop them sticking together. Repeat with the remaining batter to cook the rest, adding a little more oil to the pan every couple of pancakes, if necessary.

Once the last pancake is cooked, remove the stack of pancakes from the oven and serve immediately.

SPELT 'BUTTERMILK' PANCAKES WITH BACON, AVOCADO AND MAPLE SYRUP

1 tablespoon lemon juice
275ml almond milk
120g wholegrain spelt flour
160g self-raising flour
½ teaspoon bicarbonate of soda
Generous pinch of sea salt
2 eggs
50g dairy-free sunflower spread,
   melted and cooled
Sunflower or vegetable oil,
   for frying

TO SERVE
8 rashers of streaky bacon
2 avocados, sliced
Maple syrup, to drizzle

Serves 4

No one should have to live without pancakes and luckily you don't have to – there are lots of dairy-free substitutes to use in your batter. For a start, you can recreate the slightly sour tang of buttermilk by adding lemon juice to almond milk. Use this 'buttermilk' to make classic American pancakes, with just a hint of worthiness (hello, wholegrain spelt flour). Stack 'em high and drizzle with maple syrup. (See photograph on page 14.)

Add the lemon juice to the almond milk, stir and leave to rest for 5 minutes. Meanwhile, sift both flours into a large bowl. Fold in the bicarbonate of soda and salt, using a large metal spoon. Form a well in the centre.

Whisk the eggs and almond milk mixture together. Pour into the well a little at a time, whisking as you go to incorporate. When you've added about half, add the melted sunflower spread and whisk to combine. Add the rest of the almond milk and keep whisking until you have a thick, smooth batter. Leave the mixture to rest for 10 minutes and preheat the oven to its lowest setting.

Heat a non-stick frying pan over a medium-high heat. Before it gets too hot, drizzle a little oil into the pan and use kitchen paper to evenly grease the bottom and remove the excess. Once the pan has heated up, ladle 3 tablespoons of the batter into the pan per pancake and swirl into a circle. You will be able to fit about 2 pancakes into your pan at one time. Cook for 2–3 minutes, until bubbles start to form on the surface and the edges start to lift away from the pan. Flip over using a spatula and cook for 1–2 minutes on the other side, until golden and cooked through.

Repeat in batches until you've used up all the batter (you may need to add a little more oil after every couple of pancakes) and keep the pancakes warm on a plate in the low oven, layering each with a sheet of kitchen paper.

Meanwhile, heat a separate frying pan over a medium-high heat and fry the bacon until it reaches your preferred state of crispiness.

Once all the pancakes are cooked, divide them into stacks between four plates. Top with the crispy bacon, drizzle maple syrup over the top and serve with the avocado.

BAKED EGGS WITH WILTED SPINACH, PROSCIUTTO AND TRUFFLE OIL

200g baby leaf spinach
4 slices prosciutto
8 large eggs
A few drops of truffle oil
4 large slices sourdough bread
Dairy-free sunflower spread
Sea salt and freshly ground
    black pepper

8 ramekin dishes, greased with
    vegetable oil

Serves 4

Baked eggs are a brunch staple. They're perfect for mornings when your co-ordination is AWOL after a few drinks the night before, as there's none of the timing, whisking, juggling fandango of eggs Benedict, but all of the deliciousness. The eggs will be ready in the time it takes you to toast some sourdough and put a pot of strong espresso on the stove.

Preheat the oven to 180°C/350°F/Gas Mark 4.

Wash the spinach, remove any tough stalks and put into a large saucepan. Just cover with water and simmer for about 3 minutes until wilted. Drain and pat dry with kitchen paper, squeezing to remove any excess water.

Place a little spinach in the bottom of each greased ramekin. Tear each slice of prosciutto in two, then place one piece in the bottom of each ramekin with the spinach. Sprinkle a little salt and pepper on top.

Break an egg into each ramekin. Add a drop or two of truffle oil to each dish and an extra grind of pepper on top. Place the ramekins in a roasting tin and then pour boiling water into the tin to come about halfway up the ramekins (this water bath will stop the eggs drying out). Bake in the oven for 10–12 minutes until the eggs are just set but the yolks are still wobbly.

Meanwhile, toast the sourdough bread, butter with your favourite dairy-free spread and cut into soldiers to dunk into the eggs. Serve two ramekins per person, along with some soldiers.

EGGS BENEDICT

2 English muffins, split in half
4 eggs
4 slices good-quality ham,
    such as Yorkshire

**FOR THE SORT-OF
HOLLANDAISE**
2 egg yolks
1 tablespoon white wine vinegar
120g dairy-free sunflower spread,
    melted
1 teaspoon lemon juice
Small bunch of tarragon, leaves
    only, finely chopped
Sea salt and freshly ground
    black pepper

Serves 2

Brunch is a minefield for the dairy-free. Everything on the menu sounds delicious, but the granola is smothered in yogurt, the pancakes are full of milk and as for the eggs Benedict – there's a lake of clarified butter in the hollandaise. I was initially nervous about making this butterific dish dairy-free, but was delighted with the results I got with sunflower spread. It tastes absolutely as good as the real thing...

For the sort-of hollandaise, place a heatproof bowl over a pan of gently simmering water set over a low heat, making sure the bowl doesn't touch the water. Add the egg yolks and vinegar to the bowl and whisk constantly until thickened. Slowly pour in the melted spread, whisking continuously. If the sauce looks like it's about to curdle, remove the bowl from the heat for a minute and keep whisking, before returning to the pan. When the sauce is thickened and glossy, remove from the heat, whisk in the lemon juice and season to taste. Whisk in the tarragon leaves and cover with a tea towel to keep warm.

Meanwhile, toast the muffin halves (it definitely helps to put your breakfasting companion to work here – that way they can assemble the rest of the dish while you stand guard whisking the hollandaise) and poach the eggs (see page 32).

Place two toasted muffin halves on each plate. Spread a little hollandaise on each, then top with a folded slice of the ham, then a poached egg. Drizzle the hollandaise on top and serve.

FOUR BUTTER-FREE THINGS ON TOAST

1. AVOCADO AND SMOKED SALMON ON RYE

1 ripe avocado
1 teaspoon extra-virgin olive oil
1-2 slices good rye bread per
    person
4 slices smoked salmon
Squeeze of lemon juice
Sea salt and freshly ground
    black pepper

Serves 2

Ten years ago, avocado on toast was a fringe notion – now it's every savvy breakfast and bruncher's topping of choice. Creamy avocado mashed with good olive oil and topped with delicate slivers of smoked salmon is a delicious, and protein-packed, way to start your day.

Slice the avocado in half, remove the stone and scoop the flesh into a small bowl. Pour in the oil and mash with the back of a fork until all the large lumps are broken up. Add salt and pepper to taste.

Toast the rye bread and spread with the mashed avocado. Fold the slices of smoked salmon on top. Squeeze a little lemon juice on top of the salmon and finish with an extra grind of black pepper.

2. CASHEW BUTTER, BANANA AND HONEY ON WHOLEGRAIN

This is less a recipe, more a recommendation for a delicious combination for topping thick slices of lightly toasted wholegrain toast. Calcium-packed cashew butter has a mild, distinct flavour that is very different to peanut butter. Top with slices of banana and a drizzle of honey. Scatter a few sesame seeds on top for an extra calcium boost.

3. HOMEMADE CHOCOLATE AND HAZELNUT SPREAD, AKA 'NOTELLA'

200g blanched hazelnuts
100g dark chocolate
150ml coconut cream, plus extra
  to taste
½ teaspoon vanilla extract
1 tablespoon maple syrup
Pinch of sea salt
3 tablespoons sunflower oil

Makes 1 small jar

Whether you like it spread on toast, smeared on top of waffles or hidden inside a crêpe, chocolate and hazelnut spread (its Italian name is *gianduja*) is irresistible stuff. This homemade version is more intense than the bought stuff as it's made with dark chocolate; stir a little extra coconut cream in at the end if you want a milkier taste.

Toast the hazelnuts in a small, dry frying pan over a medium-high heat until they start to turn golden and release their toasty hazelnut aroma. Keep a careful eye on them as they can burn quickly. Tip onto a plate and leave to cool.

Finely chop the chocolate and place in a large, lipped bowl.

Heat the coconut cream in a small saucepan over a medium-high heat. Remove from the heat just before it starts to boil – when you start to see bubbles form around the edges.

Pour the cream over the chocolate and stir gently with a wooden spoon until all the chocolate has melted and you have a smooth ganache. (If there is still a little chocolate which hasn't melted, then fill the empty saucepan with water and bring to a simmer – set the glass mixing bowl above the saucepan so it isn't touching the water and melt the last of the chocolate, stirring gently.) Add the vanilla and maple syrup and stir again until combined.

Blitz the toasted hazelnuts in a food processor until they break down first into ground nuts. Add the salt and blitz again. Keep scraping down the sides of the food processor with a spatula. Slowly trickle in the oil with the motor running, then keep going until you have a thick liquid consistency, similar to peanut butter – this will take 3-4 minutes. Depending on the strength of your food processor you may not be able to break the nuts down entirely, but don't worry, it will still taste delicious.

Stir the nut mixture into the ganache and leave to cool completely. Stir in an extra tablespoon or 2 of coconut cream if you would like it a little milkier.

Spoon into an airtight, sterilised jar. It will keep in the fridge for several weeks, should you be able to resist snarfing it all in one go.

4. HOMEMADE BAKED BEANS

2 tablespoons olive oil
1 onion, finely diced
1 garlic clove, crushed
400g tin chopped tomatoes
1 tablespoon dark muscovado
  sugar
1 tablespoon black treacle
2 teaspoons English mustard
1 tablespoon cider vinegar
400g tin haricot beans, rinsed
  and drained
Few drops of Tabasco or Sriracha
  (optional)
Sea salt and freshly ground
  black pepper

Serves 4

It may seem counter-intuitive to use a tin of beans to make baked beans, but trust me on this. Proper, home-cooked baked beans have about as much in common with the ready-made ones as supermarket sushi has with Tokyo's finest. Instead of a thin, neon-orange sauce, you get a complex dish with the pucker of vinegar, the depth of black treacle and the heat of mustard. It's delicious with poached eggs and sausages or crispy bacon, and even with shredded Savoy cabbage stirred through.

Heat a large, heavy-bottomed saucepan over a low-medium heat and add the oil. Add the onion and cook for about 5 minutes until softened, before adding the garlic and cooking for another minute.

Pour in the chopped tomatoes, then add the sugar, treacle, mustard and vinegar and stir to combine. Simmer for a few minutes over a medium heat before adding the beans and salt and pepper to taste. Reduce the heat to low and partially cover with a lid.

Simmer for 1 hour over a low heat, stirring the beans periodically. If the sauce looks like it's becoming too thick and the beans are in danger of sticking to the pot, add a little water to loosen the mixture.

Adjust the seasoning and add a few drops of Tabasco or Sriracha if you like more heat.

CHOCOLATE AND BLUEBERRY PORRIDGE WITH TOASTED ALMONDS

50g porridge oats
220ml almond milk or vanilla
  rice milk
3 teaspoons cocoa powder
2 teaspoons maple syrup or
  agave nectar
50g blueberries, plus extra
  to sprinkle
Small handful of toasted flaked
  almonds, to sprinkle

Serves 1

Porridge is one of the best ways to start the day (sorry, bacon). But to keep eating it every weekday morning, I need some fun ingredients. Enter: chocolate. More precisely, cocoa powder – adding Galaxy bars wouldn't exactly get the day off to a nourishing, dairy-free start. As the porridge heats up, add some blueberries. They'll start to soften and burst, releasing their indigo juices. The whole thing takes less than 10 minutes and makes early mornings bearable.

Place the oats in a small saucepan and add the almond or rice milk. Add the cocoa powder and maple syrup or agave nectar, stirring until the lumps of cocoa have broken up and are blended in.

Heat for a couple of minutes over a low-medium heat, stirring regularly. Add the blueberries after a few minutes; this way they will start to burst but won't lose their shape completely. Bring to the boil briefly, then reduce the heat and simmer for 3–4 minutes, stirring well.

Serve with a few extra blueberries and toasted flaked almonds sprinkled on top.

CACAO NIB AND CRANBERRY GRANOLA

100ml maple syrup
2 teaspoons coconut oil
150ml apple juice
1 teaspoon ground cinnamon
375g jumbo rolled oats
100g pecans, roughly chopped
50g pumpkin seeds
50g sesame seeds
Pinch of sea salt
75g dried cranberries
75g cacao nibs

Makes 700g

Granola is both easy and fun to make at home (rainy day cooking project alert!). Making it yourself also means you can control what's in it. The dried cranberries in this recipe are both sweet and a little tart at the same time, while cacao nibs add a decadent hint of chocolate but are sugar-free and packed full of nutrients. Eat with almond or rice milk, or use in the Bircher Muesli Sundaes (see page 38).

Preheat the oven to 150°C/300°F/Gas Mark 2. Heat the maple syrup, coconut oil and apple juice in a saucepan over a medium heat, stirring occasionally with a wooden spoon, until the oil has melted and the mixture is well combined.

Grease and line a baking tray.

Put the cinnamon, oats, pecans, seeds and salt into a large bowl. Pour in the syrup mixture and stir to coat. Spread this mixture out over the prepared baking tray, pinching some of it together with your fingers to form small granola clusters.

Bake in the oven for 45 minutes, or until golden brown. Remove from the oven and leave to cool on the baking tray. Once it is completely cool, stir in the dried cranberries and cacao nibs. Store in a sterilised Kilner jar or airtight tin. It will keep for several weeks. Serve with coconut yogurt, if you like.

BREAKFAST BURRITOS

½ tablespoon olive oil
1 round shallot, finely diced
½ red chilli, finely diced
½ teaspoon ground cumin
225g firm tofu, drained and
    patted dry
8 cherry tomatoes, quartered
30g baby leaf spinach
4 medium corn tortillas
1 avocado, halved and finely
    sliced
Small handful of fresh coriander
    leaves, chopped
Few drops of Tabasco
1 lime, cut into wedges
Sea salt and freshly ground
    black pepper

Serves 2 (makes 4)

Burritos for breakfast – sounds seriously unhealthy, right? Not when we're talking warm corn tortillas filled with scrambled tofu, baby spinach, cherry tomatoes and creamy avocado. The perkiness of the lime and Tabasco is as good as a caffeine hit.

Heat the oil in a large, heavy-bottomed frying pan over a medium heat. Add the shallot and chilli and fry gently for around 3 minutes, until the shallot has softened and is turning translucent. Add the cumin and fry for just 30 seconds, until fragrant.

Add the tofu to the pan. Fry for 3-4 minutes, until cooked through, using a wooden spoon to break it up until it resembles scrambled eggs. Add the tomatoes and spinach and cook for a further 2 minutes, then season generously and remove from the heat.

Meanwhile, place a small frying pan over a high heat. Add the tortillas one at a time and toast for around 30 seconds on each side until they start to turn golden.

Place a quarter of the tofu, spinach and tomato mixture onto the middle of each tortilla. Add the avocado slices, sprinkle over a little coriander and add a few drops of Tabasco and a squeeze of lime. Fold the sides of the tortilla into the centre, on top of the filling. Take the bottom of the tortilla and lift it over the filling, and then roll up. Eat immediately.

CHORIZO AND CHARGRILLED PEPPER MUFFINS

A little olive oil
60g chorizo, cut into small dice
275g self-raising flour
1 teaspoon baking powder
½ teaspoon bicarbonate of soda
½ teaspoon smoked paprika
Pinch of sea salt
1 egg
125ml sunflower oil
100ml soya or almond milk
150g plain soya yogurt
130g chargrilled peppers from
    a jar, cut into 1cm dice

12-hole muffin tray lined with
    12 muffin cases

Makes 12

Chorizo makes everything taste better. Even a small hit of its intensely piggy, spicy flavour lifts stews, soups and all manner of eggy brunch dishes from average to incredible in the amount of time it takes you to dribble hot, ochre chorizo juice down your chin. My current favourite way of shoehorning chorizo into even more dishes is adding it to savoury baked goods like these easy muffins: a hint of backstreet tapas bar at breakfast time.

Heat a few drops of olive oil in a frying pan over a medium heat. Add the diced chorizo and fry until crispy. Using a slotted spoon, remove to a plate lined with a few sheets of kitchen paper to absorb excess oil, and leave to cool completely.

Preheat the oven to 200°C/400°F/Gas Mark 6. Using a large metal spoon, fold the flour, baking powder, bicarbonate of soda, smoked paprika and salt together in a large bowl, until just combined.

Beat the egg, sunflower oil, soya or almond milk and soya yogurt in a separate bowl, using a fork, until they form a smooth batter. Pour into the dry ingredients and fold in with a large metal spoon, just until the wet ingredients are incorporated; don't overwork the batter. Add the cooled chorizo and diced red pepper and fold in until just combined.

Spoon into the muffin cases and bake in the oven for 15-20 minutes, or until the tops are golden. Leave to cool on a wire rack, in the cases, for 5-10 minutes, before serving warm.

COURGETTE FRITTERS
WITH POACHED EGGS

1-2 eggs per person
Hot sauce or chilli sauce

FOR THE FRITTERS
100g fine polenta
1 teaspoon (gluten-free) baking
    powder
½ teaspoon smoked paprika
2 eggs
2 courgettes (around 400g in
    total), coarsely grated
1 red chilli, deseeded and finely
    diced
1 spring onion (white and green
    part), finely sliced
6 tablespoons vegetable,
    sunflower or groundnut oil
Sea salt and freshly ground
    black pepper

Serves 4 (makes about 10)

These courgette fritters get extra crunch from being made with polenta instead of flour (which makes them gluten-free to boot). They make a fine weekend breakfast, drizzled with hot sauce and topped with a poached egg. We've also been known to eat them as 'breakfast for dinner', washed down with an ice-cold beer.

Preheat the oven to its lowest setting. Mix together the polenta, baking powder, smoked paprika and eggs with a fork. Pat the grated courgettes dry with kitchen paper, then stir these into the mixture. Stir in the chilli and spring onion and season.

Heat the oil in a large, heavy-bottomed frying pan over a medium-high heat. Once hot, spoon in heaped dessertspoonfuls of the batter and pat down gently into discs, 2-3 at a time so the pan doesn't become overcrowded. Fry for 2-3 minutes, until golden on the bottom, then flip over with a fish slice and cook the other side for a 2-3 minutes. You may need to add a little more oil to the pan between each batch.

Keep warm in the oven on a plate lined with kitchen paper until all the fritters are cooked, layering kitchen paper between each to help soak up oil and keep them crisp.

Meanwhile, poach the eggs. There's the proper way to make poached eggs, and the cheat's way. Here are both:

PROPER WAY: Firstly, use a very fresh egg. Then take a tip from food writer Felicity Cloake and break the egg into a small jug, and add a drop of white wine vinegar. Bring a saucepan of water to the boil, then whisk the water vigorously to create a whirlpool effect. Stop whisking, then immediately and carefully pour the egg into the centre of the whirlpool. Reduce the heat slightly and simmer for 3 minutes.

CHEAT'S WAY: Line a ramekin with a square of clingfilm about the size of a piece of kitchen paper. Grease with a little oil using your fingertip, then break an egg into it. Gather up the sides and twist the top to secure. Repeat for as many eggs as you need. Lower these carefully into a pan of simmering water and poach for 4 minutes.

Serve the fritters in small stacks, topped with a poached egg and perhaps a few drops of chilli sauce or your favourite hot sauce.

BLACK FOREST WAFFLES WITH MORELLO CHERRY COMPOTE AND MACADAMIA CREAM

175g plain flour
50g wholegrain spelt flour
1½ teaspoons baking powder
Pinch of sea salt
25g cocoa powder
3 tablespoons caster sugar
3 eggs
450ml almond milk
85g dairy-free sunflower spread,
   melted and cooled
Vegetable oil, for greasing
35g dark chocolate chips

FOR THE MACADAMIA CREAM
200g blanched macadamia nuts
275ml cold, filtered water
½ teaspoon vanilla extract
1½ teaspoons maple syrup
Pinch of sea salt

FOR THE COMPOTE
400g frozen morello cherries
   or forest fruits
1 tablespoon caster sugar
200ml water

Waffle maker or stovetop
   waffle iron

Serves 4

Frozen Black Forest gateau, with its curls of cheap chocolate and turrets of cream, was a favourite childhood treat of mine. It's long since fallen from fashion, but Black Forest's trinity of chocolate, cherries and cream is evergreen. These Black Forest waffles are definitely a special-occasion breakfast. The gooey cocoa batter is flecked with nibs of melting dark chocolate, served with a juicy cherry compote and a big dollop of chilled macadamia cream.

For the macadamia cream, the night before, place the macadamias in a large bowl. Add enough cold water from the tap to cover the nuts, cover the bowl and leave to soak overnight.

The next morning, rinse and drain the nuts and put them in a blender with the 275ml filtered water. Add the vanilla, maple syrup and salt and blitz until you have a thick cream, then refrigerate until needed.

For the waffles, sift both flours, the baking powder, salt, cocoa powder and sugar into a large bowl. Beat the eggs, almond milk and cooled, melted spread together. Whisk into the flour mixture and continue whisking until you have a smooth, lump-free batter. Leave to stand for 10 minutes. Preheat the oven to its lowest setting.

Make the compote by putting the frozen fruits, sugar and water into a saucepan. Bring to the boil briefly, then turn the heat down slightly and simmer until the fruits have softened and you have a thick compote. Remove from the heat and cover to keep warm.

Preheat the waffle maker or the stovetop waffle iron, and lightly grease with vegetable oil. Stir the chocolate chips into the rested batter, then ladle in the correct amount of batter for your hot waffle maker, making sure you ladle out a few chocolate chips for each waffle if they have sunk to the bottom. Cook until crisp on the outside, and keep warm on a plate lined with kitchen paper in the low oven while you make the rest of the waffles.

Serve in stacks with a big dollop of the macadamia cream and the compote on the side.

CHAI FRENCH TOAST WITH CINNAMON-ROASTED PEARS

225ml almond or vanilla
　　rice milk
4 eggs
1½ tablespoons golden caster
　　sugar
1 teaspoon ground ginger
½ teaspoon ground cinnamon
2 cardamom pods, lightly
　　crushed
1 teaspoon ground nutmeg
2 cloves
Pinch of sea salt and a generous
　　twist of black pepper
4 thick slices of slightly stale,
　　good white bread
2 tablespoons sunflower or
　　rapeseed oil
Granulated sugar, to sprinkle
Coconut yogurt, to serve

FOR THE PEARS

1 tablespoon light olive oil, plus
　　extra for greasing
2 teaspoons soft brown sugar
1 teaspoon ground cinnamon
1 teaspoon vanilla extract
4 small pears, peeled, halved
　　lengthways and pips removed

Serves 4

Golden-crusted French toast, scented with chai spices. Pair it (forgive the pun) with juicy roasted pears and you have a recipe for pure breakfast indulgence.

Whisk together the almond or rice milk, eggs, sugar, spices, salt and pepper in a mixing jug and leave to infuse while you make the pears.

Preheat the oven to 180°C/350°F/Gas Mark 4. Line a baking tray with foil and drizzle with a few drops of olive oil.

For the pears, mix together the oil, sugar, cinnamon and vanilla in a bowl. Toss the pear halves in this mixture to coat. Place on the foil-lined tray, drizzle with any remaining cinnamon mixture and roast in the preheated oven for 25 minutes or until golden, and tender in the middle, turning them over halfway through cooking. Remove from the oven and cover with foil to keep warm while you make the custard mixture.

Pour the milk and egg mixture into a medium-sized baking dish and pick out the whole spices. Whisk again to make sure the spices don't cling to the side of the dish. Lay the slices of bread in the liquid and soak for 30 seconds, pressing down lightly with a wooden spoon. Turn over and soak the other side for 30-60 seconds (you may need to do this in batches, depending on the size of your dish). Transfer to a plate.

Heat the oil a large, heavy-bottomed frying pan over a medium-high heat. Add a slice of the soaked bread and fry for about 3 minutes, until golden on the bottom. Don't move it during this time, so it can form a good crust. Sprinkle the top with a little granulated sugar, then flip over and cook the other side until golden. Transfer to a plate and cover with foil to keep warm while you repeat with the remaining slices of soaked bread.

Serve with two pear halves on top of each slice of toast, and a dollop of coconut yogurt.

APRICOT AND PISTACHIO BREAKFAST BREAD

70g shelled pistachio kernels
150g self-raising flour, sifted
75g polenta
1 teaspoon baking powder
Pinch of salt
125g dried apricots, finely
    diced into approximately
    3-mm cubes
245ml olive oil
200g golden caster sugar
4 eggs

900g/2lb loaf tin

Makes 1 large loaf

Bake this simple loaf cake ahead of time when you're expecting a crowd for brunch. Leftovers can be sliced and frozen, then toasted under the grill and spread with a little coconut oil or coconut butter. The polenta adds texture and a little crunch, and the loaf is flecked with sweet apricots and delicious toasted pistachios.

Toast the pistachio kernels in a dry frying pan over a medium heat, until they start to turn golden (keep a careful eye on them as they can easily burn). Remove to a plate and leave to cool. Once completely cool, roughly chop into small pieces.

Grease and line the loaf tin with greaseproof paper.

Preheat the oven to 180°C/350°F/Gas Mark 4.

Sift the flour, polenta, baking powder and salt together in a large bowl. Scoop out 2 tablespoons of this mixture and use to coat the apricot and pistachio pieces; this is important to stop the fruit and nuts sinking in the cake batter. Set aside.

Beat the olive oil and sugar together with an electric whisk in another large bowl or with the paddle attachment of a stand mixer for a couple of minutes, until well combined.

Add the eggs one at a time, alternating with a tablespoon of the flour mixture, and keep whisking to combine.

Fold in the rest of the flour mixture using a large metal spoon, until just combined. Fold in the flour-covered apricots and pistachios.

Pour the mixture into the loaf tin and smooth the top. Bake for 50–60 minutes, or until the top is golden and a skewer or cocktail stick inserted into the middle comes out clean. Leave to cool in the tin for 5 minutes before turning out onto a wire rack to cool completely.

Serve with a dollop of coconut yogurt. Slice any leftover breakfast bread and freeze.

BIRCHER MUESLI SUNDAES

150g whole rolled oats
2 tablespoons flaked almonds,
  chopped
2 tablespoons lemon juice
200ml water
150g coconut yogurt
1 teaspoon maple syrup or honey
  (optional)
Granola (see cacao nib and
  cranberry granola on page 28)
Fresh blueberries
Fresh strawberries, sliced

1 tall sundae/knickerbocker glory
  glass per person

*Serves 4–6, depending on the
  size of your glasses*

There aren't many dishes served in sundae glasses that can be legitimately called healthy, but here's one. I got the idea for these from a sweet, 1950s-style café in Melbourne, where they serve Bircher and blackberries in tall glasses, to be eaten with a long sundae spoon and washed down with a strong coffee.

The night before, mix the oats and flaked almonds together with the lemon juice and water in a large bowl. Cover and leave in the fridge.

The next morning, stir the coconut yogurt into the mixture to make the Bircher. Sweeten with the maple syrup or honey, if you like, but remember that the granola and berries will both bring sweetness to the dish.

Make sundaes by layering alternate layers of Bircher muesli, granola and berries in each sundae glass. Top with a final layer of berries and a scattering of flaked almonds, and eat with long sundae spoons.

DAIRY-FREE MILKS

Make your own milks, if you can, as most bought versions contain oils and stabilisers. If using almond milk in cooking, keep it plain with a pinch of salt; if not then it is much yummier with a little maple or agave syrup or honey, and spices like cinnamon and nutmeg. Cashew milk is – in my opinion – the most delicious. When boosted by vanilla, maple and sea salt, it has a pleasant, biscuity taste. The oat milk will turn out creamier and thicker than a shop-bought one and it benefits from a little maple syrup and vanilla. Rice milk is a little thin to use in cooking but it works well on cereal and in drinks. Please note, the NHS in the UK does not recommend rice milk for children under 5 years. For all the milks except the rice one, you can use the meal left behind in the sieve to stir into bircher muesli, porridge, smoothies or coconut yogurt.

ALMOND MILK

200g whole unsalted almonds, skin on
600ml cold, filtered water
Pinch of sea salt

FOR SWEETENED MILK
1 tablespoon maple syrup
½ teaspoon ground cinnamon and/or nutmeg
1½ teaspoons vanilla extract

Makes about 500ml (use the ratio of 1:3 nuts to water to make more or less milk)

Place the almonds in a large bowl. Add enough cold tap water to cover the nuts, cover the bowl and leave to soak for 8 hours or overnight.

Drain the almonds and rinse well. Place in a blender and add the cold, filtered water and the salt. Add the maple syrup, cinnamon or nutmeg and vanilla, if making sweetened milk. Blitz until the almonds are broken up into very small pieces and you have a creamy liquid. Place a fine-mesh sieve over a large bowl and line with a piece of muslin. Pour the almond milk mixture into the muslin-lined sieve and press down firmly with a spoon to push all the liquid through into the bowl, leaving the nut meal in the sieve. If the milk still has bits of nuts in it, pour it back through the sieve. Store in an airtight container in the fridge for a couple of days. Shake well before using.

RICE MILK

200g brown or white rice
600ml cold, filtered water
Pinch of sea salt

FOR SWEETENED MILK
1 tablespoon maple syrup
1½ tablespoons vanilla extract

Makes about 600ml (use the ratio of 1:3 rice to water to make more or less milk)

Place the rice in a large bowl and cover with double the volume of cold tap water. Leave to soak for 8 hours or overnight.

The next day, drain and thoroughly rinse the rice. Place the rice in a blender and add the filtered water and the salt. Add the maple syrup and vanilla, if making sweetened milk. Blitz until the rice is broken up into very small pieces and you have a creamy liquid. Place a fine-mesh sieve over a large mixing bowl and line with a piece of muslin. Pour the liquid and rice meal into the muslin-lined sieve. Press down firmly with a spoon to push the last of the liquid into the bowl, leaving the rice meal behind. Discard the rice.

OAT MILK

200g porridge oats (look for gluten-free oats if you want to ensure this is gluten-free, too)
600ml cold, filtered water
Pinch of sea salt

FOR SWEETENED MILK
1 tablespoon maple syrup
½ teaspoon ground cinnamon and/or nutmeg
1½ teaspoons vanilla extract

Makes about 500ml (use the ratio of 1:3 oats to water to make more or less milk)

Soak the oats in the filtered water for 1 hour. Strain the liquid into a blender, then rinse the softened oats before adding them to the blender with the salt. Add the maple syrup, spices and vanilla, if making sweetened milk. Blitz until smooth.

Place a fine-mesh sieve over a large mixing bowl. Pour the oat mixture into the sieve and press down with a wooden spoon to push all the liquid through the oats into the bowl. Transfer the oat mixture to a separate bowl and use to make porridge. If the oat milk still has pieces of oats in it, you can pour it back through the sieve. Use on porridge and cereal, and in smoothies and drinks. It keeps for up to a week in an airtight container in the fridge. Shake well before using.

CASHEW MILK

200g unsalted cashew nuts
600ml cold, filtered water
Pinch of sea salt
1 tablespoon maple syrup
1½ teaspoons vanilla extract

Makes around 500ml (use the ratio of 1:3 nuts to water to make more or less milk)

Put the cashews in a large bowl. Add enough cold tap water to cover the nuts, cover the bowl and leave to soak for 8 hours or overnight.

Drain the cashews, rinse well and place in a blender. Add the cold, filtered water, salt, maple syrup, and vanilla (or for unsweetened milk, omit these last two). Blitz until the cashews are broken up into very small pieces and you have a pale, creamy liquid. Place a fine-mesh sieve over a large bowl and line with a piece of muslin. Pour the cashew milk mixture into the muslin-lined sieve and press down firmly with a spoon to push all the liquid through into the bowl, leaving the nut meal in the sieve. If the milk still has bits of nuts in it, pour it back through the sieve. Store in an airtight container in the fridge for a couple of days. Shake well before using.

ALTERNATIVES: To make chocolate milk, add 2 teaspoons cocoa powder to the blender with the nuts, water, salt, maple syrup and vanilla (omit the spices). To make gingerbread milk, add 1½ teaspoons ground ginger and ½ teaspoon ground nutmeg to the blender with the nuts, water, salt, maple syrup and vanilla.

LUNCH

ULTIMATE FISH FINGER SANDWICH WITH CHIPOTLE MAYO AND ROCKET

FOR THE FISH FINGERS
200g sustainable white fish
    fillets, such as pollack
40g plain flour
1 egg, beaten
70g panko breadcrumbs
3 tablespoons vegetable or
    sunflower oil
Sea salt and freshly ground
    black pepper

FOR THE SANDWICHES
1 teaspoon chipotle paste
2 tablespoons good-quality
    mayonnaise (check the label
    to make sure it's dairy free)
4 slices white sourdough bread
1 handful of fresh rocket

Serves 2

The fish finger sandwich is a British classic. Food historians trace its roots back to the 1980s, the golden era of frozen dinners and suspiciously orange breadcrumbs. It was a time when we weren't afraid to double-carb by stuffing fish fingers inside bendy white bread. As much as shop-bought fish fingers are still a guilty pleasure, homemade ones, coated in crisp panko and sandwiched between fresh sourdough, are in another league altogether.

Preheat the oven to its lowest setting.

Skin the fish fillets if necessary and cut into strips 2–3cm wide, using a sharp knife.

Mix the flour with some salt and pepper on a plate. Put the bowl of beaten egg next to it, the panko breadcrumbs on another plate next to that, and finally a clean plate. Using kitchen tongs, roll the fish strips in the seasoned flour to coat. Shake off any excess and then carefully dip in the beaten egg with the tongs, before rolling in the panko breadcrumbs – each 'finger' should be thoroughly coated with the breadcrumbs. Place the fish fingers on the clean plate.

Heat the oil in a large, heavy-bottomed frying pan over a high heat. Test whether the oil is hot enough by dropping in a breadcrumb – it should start sizzling immediately. Add the fish fingers to the hot oil and fry in a couple of batches for 2–3 minutes on each side until the breadcrumbs are crisp and golden and the fish is cooked through. Use the kitchen tongs to lift the fish fingers and brown the sides. Keep the first batch warm on a plate in the low oven.

Meanwhile, mix the chipotle paste and mayonnaise together in a bowl. Cut the sourdough slices in half and spread the chipotle mayo on each. Add a small handful of rocket to one half, top with a couple of fish fingers and the other half slice of bread. Serve immediately.

CAESAR SALAD

2 tablespoons olive oil
1-2 slices sourdough or good-
    quality white bread, cut into
    2cm cubes
1 large Cos or Romaine lettuce,
    divided into leaves
1 tablespoon toasted flaked
    almonds
Sea salt and freshly ground
    black pepper

FOR THE DRESSING
1 ½ teaspoons Worcestershire
    sauce
2 anchovy fillets in oil, chopped
1 garlic clove
Finely grated zest of 1 lemon
    and the juice of ½
4 tablespoons good-quality
    mayonnaise (check the label
    to make sure it's dairy-free)

Serves 4

There was a time in the 1990s and noughties when you couldn't avoid Caesar salad. It may not have the fashion clout of kale and quinoa, but a good Caesar is still just as delicious as it was back then. Here, toasted flaked almonds take the place of Parmesan, and the creamy dressing makes eating a big plate of lettuce a pleasure. For a more substantial salad, add pieces of grilled chicken and/or crispy bacon.

Heat the oil in a small, heavy-bottomed frying pan over a medium-high heat. Add the bread cubes, sprinkle with salt and fry until golden, using kitchen tongs to turn them over to ensure all sides are cooked. Transfer to a plate lined with kitchen paper and set aside.

To make the dressing, blitz the Worcestershire sauce, chopped anchovies, garlic and lemon zest in a small food processor (you want a paste, but some texture is fine). Spoon into a bowl and add the lemon juice and mayonnaise. Whisk until you have a smooth dressing, then season to taste.

Toss the dressing with the lettuce and flaked almonds in a bowl until well coated. Divide between four plates, top with the croûtons and serve.

COUSCOUS WITH TOASTED ALMONDS AND CRISPY KALE

2 tablespoons olive oil
250g couscous
Finely grated zest of 1 lemon
400ml hot chicken or vegetable
    stock
100g curly kale, any woody
    stalks removed
50g toasted flaked almonds
Sea salt

FOR THE DRESSING
3 tablespoons extra-virgin
    olive oil
1 tablespoon lemon juice
½ tablespoon soy sauce

Serves 4

This easy side dish packs a lot of flavour thanks to the salty, crispy kale, lemon zest and the secret ingredient in the dressing: soy sauce. Make it a filling meal by serving with chicken drumsticks or sausages. Any leftovers will keep in the fridge for lunchboxes the following day.

Heat 1 tablespoon of the oil in a large, heavy-bottomed pan (that has a lid) over a medium-high heat. Add the couscous and fry gently for 2 minutes, stirring to coat all the grains.

Add the lemon zest, then pour in the stock. Stir once, then remove from the heat, cover and leave for 5-10 minutes.

Meanwhile, heat the remaining tablespoon of oil in a heavy-bottomed frying pan. Add the curly kale, sprinkle with salt and stir-fry until dark and crispy, for about 5 minutes.

Whisk together the dressing ingredients. Pour over the couscous and stir, before adding the crispy kale and almonds. Serve immediately.

PULLED PORK BELLY CEMITAS

FOR THE PULLED
PORK BELLY

800g pork belly joint
1 tablespoon olive oil
1 tablespoon sea salt
1 tablespoon soft brown sugar
1 teaspoon chipotle paste

FOR THE CEMITAS

2 avocados
4 teaspoons lime juice
1 garlic clove, crushed
4 seeded burger buns (check the
    ingredients to make sure they
    are dairy-free)
A few sprigs of fresh papalo
    (Mexican herb) or coriander
    leaves
Sea salt

Makes 4

The *cemita* is a sandwich from Mexico's Puebla region. In its classic form, avocado, meat (beef or pork) and panela cheese, and perhaps a little salsa roja, are crammed into a seeded egg roll. With a little tinkering I've made a dairy-free version with extra flavour courtesy of pulled pork belly, shards of crackling and a little chipotle.

Preheat the oven to 200°C/400°F/Gas Mark 6.

Pat the pork belly dry with kitchen paper and score the skin using a sharp paring knife. Rub the oil into the skin and then rub half of the salt and sugar in. Turn the pork belly over and rub the rest of the salt and sugar into the other side of the meat.

Place the pork belly skin side up in a roasting tin and roast for 30 minutes, then reduce the oven temperature to 150°C/300°F/Gas Mark 2 and cook for a further 3 ½ hours. Remove from the oven and pull the meat away from the skin. It should be soft and come away easily in shreds; set aside.

Increase the oven temperature back up to 200°C/400°F/Gas Mark 6 and return the pork skin to the oven in the roasting tin. Roast until you have crispy crackling, for about 15-20 minutes. Remove from the oven and leave to cool slightly, then use a sharp knife to cut it into small pieces. Stir the chipotle paste into the shredded pork.

Mash the avocados with the lime juice and garlic, and season with a little salt. Slice and lightly grill or toast the buns.

To assemble, spread a generous amount of mashed avocado on the bottom half of each bun and just a little on the top. Arrange the pulled pork on top and sprinkle with a few pieces of crackling. Top with papalo or coriander, then with the other half of the bun.

CRISPY KALE, BUTTERNUT SQUASH AND PECAN RED-QUINOA SALAD

160g red quinoa
2 tablespoons olive oil
320g butternut squash, chopped
    into 2cm cubes
125g curly kale, woody stalks
    removed
75g pecan nuts
1 heaped teaspoon rosemary
    needles
50g dried cranberries
Sea salt

TO DRESS
2 teaspoons extra-virgin olive oil
Juice of ½ lemon

Serves 4

When I lived in NYC, our 'kitchen' was a toaster oven and a hot plate. This nourishing, simple supper was something that could be made in a couple of pans, using the colourful squashes, cranberries and nuts piled high in the local grocery store, and will always remind me of a New York fall. (See photograph on page 42.)

Place the quinoa in a saucepan and cover with twice its volume of cold water. Bring to the boil, turn the heat down, cover and simmer for 18-20 minutes, until all the water is absorbed. Once cooked, fluff up the grains using a fork.

Meanwhile, heat the oil in a large, heavy-bottomed frying pan and add the cubed butternut. Cook over a high heat for 10 minutes, then add the kale, sprinkle with salt and fry for another 10 minutes, or until the kale is crispy and the squash is cooked through.

Toast the pecans with the rosemary and a little salt in a hot, dry frying pan, until they turn golden and release wonderful, toasty aromas; keep a careful eye on them to prevent burning. Remove from the heat, roughly chop and tip onto a plate to cool.

Assemble the salad on each plate by dividing the quinoa between them and adding the kale, squash and pecans. Sprinkle with dried cranberries, dress with the oil and lemon juice, and serve.

THAI-STYLE FISHCAKES WITH CRUSHED PEAS

250g boneless salmon fillets, skinned and diced
300-350g, skinless, boneless, sustainable white fish fillets such as pollack, diced
1 garlic clove
1 teaspoon soft brown sugar
1 egg
1 teaspoon chopped fresh ginger
1 teaspoon fish sauce
1 teaspoon soy sauce
1 red chilli, deseeded and finely diced
1 spring onion (white and green part), finely chopped
2 kaffir lime leaves, very finely chopped
Small handful of fresh coriander, chopped
Groundnut, vegetable or sunflower oil, for frying
Sea salt and freshly ground black pepper

FOR THE PEAS
500g frozen peas
4 tablespoons groundnut or light olive oil
½ red chilli, deseeded and finely chopped
Juice of ½ lime
Small handful of fresh coriander (leaves and stalks), finely chopped

*Serves 4 as a main course or
8 as a starter*

Thai fishcakes (or *tod man pla*) have become a classic starter in recent decades. This recipe makes larger fishcakes for an easy main course, served on a bed of peas lightly crushed with fresh chilli and lime. If you want to serve them as a starter, just divide the mixture into 6 or 8 smaller patties. They're a boon for gluten-free guests, too, as they're one of the few fishcakes not coated in breadcrumbs...

Put all the fish with the garlic, sugar, egg, ginger, fish sauce and soy sauce in a food processor and mix to a coarse paste (it should still have some texture). Transfer to a large bowl and mix in the chilli, spring onion, lime leaves and coriander. Season generously with salt and black pepper, divide the mixture into 4 and bring together with your hands to form thick, flat, round patties.

Pour enough oil to form a 2-cm layer in a large, heavy-bottomed frying pan. Heat over a high heat until it starts to shimmer. Slide in the fishcakes with a fish slice and fry for 4-5 minutes on each side until golden on the outside and cooked through. You may need to do this in batches, depending on the size of your pan.

Meanwhile, cook the peas in a saucepan of simmering water, until tender. Drain and transfer to a bowl with the oil, chilli and lime juice. Mash lightly with a potato masher, so they still retain some texture. Stir in the coriander and season.

Serve each fishcake on top of a spoonful of crushed peas.

BANH XEO

200g rice flour, sifted
2 teaspoons ground turmeric
200ml coconut milk
Generous pinch of sea salt
250ml water
Vegetable, groundnut or
    rapeseed oil, for frying
½ onion, thinly sliced
75g shiitake mushrooms,
    thinly sliced
180g raw king prawns
150g bean sprouts
1 spring onion (white and green
    part), finely sliced on the
    diagonal

FOR THE DIPPING SAUCE
(NUOC MAM PHA)

2 tablespoons lime juice
50ml fish sauce
200ml lukewarm water
50g caster sugar
1 large red chilli, finely chopped
2 garlic cloves, finely chopped

TO SERVE

Lettuce leaves
A handful of fresh coriander,
    mint and Thai basil leaves

Serves 4

Banh xeo is a crisp and lacy pancake from Vietnam. This savoury crêpe is traditionally filled with pork and prawns (though for an easy lunch I've left out the pork), vegetables and bean sprouts. Depending on where you are in Vietnam, it is made with or without coconut milk. I was taught to make it with just water but prefer the subtle coconut flavour that comes from using a mixture of the two...

Whisk together the rice flour, turmeric, coconut milk and salt. Slowly add the water until you have a thin, lump-free batter, about the consistency of single cream. Leave to stand for 20 minutes.

Meanwhile, to make the dipping sauce, whisk together the lime juice, fish sauce and water. Add the sugar and whisk until it dissolves, then add the chilli and garlic and stir to combine. Check that all the sugar has dissolved, then leave to stand.

Heat a non-stick frying or sauté pan (that has a lid) over a medium-high heat. Heat 1 tablespoon oil, then fry the onion and mushrooms, until the onions are softened and the mushrooms are turning golden, then remove to a plate. Add the prawns to the pan and fry until pink and cooked through. Remove to the plate.

Pour a little oil into the pan, swirl the pan around, then pat with kitchen paper to give the base an even covering. Turn the heat up to high then, when the oil is very hot, pour in enough pancake batter to make a thin coating on the bottom of the pan. Swirl the pan around so the batter evenly coats the base, then add a small handful of the cooked onion, mushrooms and prawns, with some bean sprouts and spring onion. Cover the pan with a lid and cook until the pancake turns very crisp. It should be golden at the edges and coming away from the pan.

Remove the lid and use a spatula or fish slice to fold one half of the pancake over the other. Carefully slide onto a plate and serve immediately with plenty of lettuce leaves, coriander, mint and Thai basil (if you can get hold of it), with the dipping sauce in small bowls on the side. The traditional way to eat *banh xeo* is to take a lettuce leaf, pile some herbs onto it, then break off a piece of the pancake and place it inside the leaf. Roll it up like a spring roll and dip into the sauce.

AVOCADO AND RADISH QUINOA TABBOULEH

120g quinoa
150ml cold water
1 avocado, peeled and cut into
    1-cm cubes
8 radishes, finely sliced
1 stick of celery, finely sliced
1 spring onion (white and green
    part), sliced on the diagonal
1 large bunch (about 28g) of
    flat-leaf parsley (including
    stalks), finely chopped
1 teaspoon mint leaves, finely
    chopped
Finely grated zest and juice
    of ½ lemon
1 ½ tablespoons extra-virgin
    olive oil
Sea salt and freshly ground
    black pepper

*Serves 2 as a light lunch
or 4 as a side dish*

This salad, what with the quinoa and the avocado, won't win any authenticity points in Beirut, but creamy avocado and peppery radish make excellent additions to a herby tabbouleh.

Place the quinoa in a saucepan and cover with the water. Bring to the boil, then turn the heat down to medium, cover and simmer for 10-15 minutes, until the grains are plumped up and have absorbed all the water yet still retain a little crunch. Set aside to cool.

Tip the cooled quinoa into a large serving bowl. Add the avocado, radishes, celery, spring onion, parsley, mint and lemon zest. Season with salt and pepper and mix well to combine. Add the olive oil and lemon juice and stir into the salad.

CREAMY CHICKEN SOUP

1 ½ tablespoons olive oil
½ onion, finely diced
1 large leek, trimmed and finely
  sliced
2 carrots, finely diced
200g leftover roast chicken,
  skinned and cut into small
  chunks
600ml hot chicken stock
150ml oat cream
½ tablespoon mustard powder
Squeeze of lemon juice
Large handful of flat-leaf parsley,
  chopped
Sea salt and freshly ground
  black pepper

Serves 4

A filling and creamy chicken soup for rainy days, cold nights and any time you need a bit of comfort in a bowl. Use ready-cooked chicken if you don't have any left over from the weekend roast...

Heat the oil in a heavy-bottomed saucepan over a medium heat. Fry the onion gently for 3–4 minutes. Add the leek and carrots and fry for a further 10 minutes, until the vegetables are softened.

Add the chicken and pour in the stock. Bring to the boil, then reduce the heat, cover and simmer for 20 minutes.

Remove 2 large spoonfuls of the chicken and vegetables and set aside on a plate. Blitz the soup with a stick blender or in a food processor until smooth. Return to the pan, if necessary, and add the reserved chicken and vegetables, then stir in the oat cream and mustard powder.

Season generously and add the lemon juice. Stir in most of the parsley, sprinkle the rest on top and serve immediately.

PARSNIP, CARROT AND SWEET POTATO SOUP WITH SOURDOUGH CROÛTONS

FOR THE SOUP

1 ½ tablespoons vegetable or
    rapeseed oil
1 onion, diced
1 red chilli, deseeded and finely
    diced
1 ½ teaspoons smoked paprika
1 teaspoon dried oregano
800g root vegetables, a mixture
    of parsnips, carrots and sweet
    potatoes, peeled and diced
1.2 litres hot chicken or vegetable
    stock
200g red lentils
Extra-virgin olive oil, to serve
Sea salt and freshly ground
    black pepper

FOR THE CROÛTONS

3 slices day-old white sourdough
    bread
3 tablespoons vegetable or
    rapeseed oil

Serves 4

There's so much goodness in this soup. The root vegetables and red lentils are packed with vitamins and fibre, and the mixture of yellow and amber ingredients is like a bowl of sunshine on a cold, grey day. Just in case it was all seeming too worthy, you've got musky heat from the chilli and smoked paprika, a little naughtiness in the form of the golden, crunchy croûtons, and a swirl of rich olive oil to finish things off.

Heat the oil in a large, heavy-bottomed saucepan over a medium heat. Sauté the onion for 5 minutes until softened and translucent. Add the chilli and cook for 1 minute, then add the smoked paprika and oregano and cook, stirring, for 30 seconds or so, until the paprika starts to release its fragrance.

Stir in the diced root vegetables and cook for a further 2 minutes. Pour in the stock and add the lentils. Bring to the boil, then turn the heat down and simmer, covered, for about 20 minutes until all the vegetables are softened.

Season with plenty of salt and some black pepper, remove from the heat and blend to a smooth soup in a blender (you will probably need to do this in batches) or with a stick blender.

Meanwhile, heat the oil for the croûtons in a frying pan over a high heat. Test whether the oil is ready by adding one bread cube. If it starts sizzling and spitting immediately, then add the other cubes. Fry for 2-3 minutes, turning regularly with a wooden spoon or spatula, until golden. Transfer to a plate lined with kitchen paper and sprinkle with salt.

Divide the soup between four bowls. Garnish each with a swirl of extra-virgin olive oil and a handful of croûtons.

SEAFOOD CHOWDER

1 tablespoon light olive oil
1 onion, finely diced
600ml hot fish stock
300g waxy potatoes, peeled
  and cut into 1-cm cubes
400ml coconut milk
3/4 teaspoon smoked paprika
270g smoked white fish, such
  as pollack
160g responsibly-sourced
  scallops
150g raw king prawns
200g frozen sweetcorn, thawed
  and drained
Squeeze of lime
Handful of fresh coriander,
  roughly chopped, to serve
Sea salt and freshly ground
  black pepper

Serves 4-6

A velvety chowder packed with scallops and prawns, and with a hint of Mexico courtesy of the smoky heat from the paprika, the corn and freshly-squeezed lime...

Heat the oil in a large, heavy-bottomed saucepan, and fry the onion gently for a few minutes until softened.

Pour in the stock, then add the potatoes. Bring to the boil briefly, then turn the heat down and simmer until the potatoes are tender.

Stir in the coconut milk, then the smoked paprika. Flake in the smoked fish, add the scallops and prawns and simmer for about 4 minutes until they are all cooked through. Add the sweetcorn and simmer for a further minute.

Season, add a squeeze of lime and serve topped with coriander.

LEMON SOLE PARCELS
WITH RICE NOODLE SALAD

2 tablespoons soy sauce
1 tablespoon lime juice
1 tablespoon runny honey
1 tablespoon groundnut or
    rapeseed oil, plus extra
    for drizzling
4 lemon sole fillets
Lime wedges, to serve

FOR THE SALAD
100g rice vermicelli noodles
Groundnut or sesame oil,
    for drizzling
2 medium carrots, cut into
    2-cm matchsticks
1 spring onion (white and green
    part), thinly sliced on the
    diagonal
½ red chilli, deseeded and
    finely diced
Large handful of coriander
    (leaves and stalks), roughly
    chopped
2 tablespoons lime juice
1 tablespoon fish sauce
1 tablespoon soy sauce
2 teaspoons caster sugar
Large handful of salted peanuts,
    roughly chopped

Serves 4

Delicate lemon sole fillets glazed with lime, soy and honey, partnered with a Thai-style rice noodle salad. This light and easy lunch is on the table in 20 minutes.

Preheat the oven to 200°C/400°F/Gas Mark 6.

Mix the soy sauce, lime juice, honey and oil together to form a glaze. Brush a light coating of the glaze onto the top side of each sole fillet. Cut out 4 squares of foil large enough to form a parcel around each fish fillet. Drizzle a few drops of oil in each and lay a fillet on top. Drizzle any extra glaze on top. Fold the sides of the foil over the fish and scrunch together at the top to form a parcel. Place on a baking tray and bake for 10 minutes until the fish is cooked through.

Meanwhile, place the noodles in a large bowl. Pour over boiling water and leave to soak for 10 minutes, or until tender but still with some bite. Drain, rinse in cold water and drain again. Toss the noodles with a little oil. Add the carrots, spring onion, chilli and most of the coriander.

Whisk together the lime juice, fish sauce, soy sauce and sugar in a bowl. Toss this dressing into the noodles, then sprinkle with the peanuts and the remaining coriander.

To serve, squeeze a little extra lime juice from one lime wedge onto each fish fillet, and serve the remaining lime wedges on the side.

SLOW-ROASTED TOMATO AND HARISSA TART

525g ripe but firm vine tomatoes, a mixture of red and yellow, cut into 1cm slices
1 teaspoon ground cumin
1 teaspoon ground coriander
1 tablespoon olive oil
Pinch of sea salt
320g sheet of ready-made puff pastry (NOT the all-butter kind)
4 tablespoons passata
2 teaspoons harissa paste
Baby spinach leaves, to garnish

Serves 4-6

Ready-made puff pastry is a nifty standby ingredient, allowing you to make impressive tarts and pastries in a hurry. Most food writers will implore readers to use all-butter pastry, but sadly that's no use for those of us avoiding dairy. Luckily, most stores also sell puff pastry made with vegetable oil and, I'll be honest, I can barely taste the difference between the two. This simple tomato tart has a North African influence thanks to the harissa paste and the earthy coriander and cumin, which contrast nicely with the sweet jamminess of the roasted tomatoes.

Preheat the oven to 140°C/275°F/Gas Mark 1.

Mix together the sliced tomatoes, cumin and coriander in a large bowl with the oil and salt, until all the slices are nicely coated with oil and spices.

Spread out the tomato slices on a baking tray. Roast for 30 minutes until the edges are slightly crisp but the middles are still soft and juicy. Remove from the oven and set aside. Increase the oven temperature to 200°C/400°F/Gas Mark 6.

Roll out the sheet of pastry onto a baking tray and score a border 3cm in from the edge. Mix the passata and harissa paste together in a bowl, then spread this mixture on the pastry inside the border. Place the tomatoes on top haphazardly (or in neat vertical rows if you prefer), overlapping each other and staying inside the border.

Bake for 20 minutes or until cooked through and the crust is puffy and golden. Garnish with baby spinach leaves and serve with new potatoes and a crisp green salad.

ROAST CHICKEN, TOASTED HAZELNUT AND APPLE ON SOURDOUGH

50g blanched hazelnuts
3 tablespoons good-quality
  mayonnaise (check the label
  to make sure it's dairy-free)
1 ½ teaspoons lemon juice
150g leftover roast chicken,
  chopped into small chunks
Small handful of flat-leaf parsley
  leaves, chopped
½ crisp red apple, cut into
  small chunks
Handful of Little Gem lettuce
  leaves
4 slices good sourdough bread,
  sliced
Sea salt and freshly ground
  black pepper

Makes 2 large sandwiches

To make this sandwich, you're going to need some leftover roast chicken (most likely from Sunday lunch, making it the perfect Monday-blues-fighting sandwich). There are lots of delicious flavours here – the toasted hazelnuts, the tender chicken and sharpness from the red apple and lemon. If you're debating whether it's worth roasting a chicken just to make this sandwich... yes. Yes it is.

Toast the hazelnuts in a small, dry frying pan over a medium-high heat until they turn golden and start to crack – keep a careful eye on them as they can burn quickly. Tip onto a plate and leave to cool before roughly chopping.

Mix the mayonnaise and lemon juice together in a large bowl and season to taste. Stir in the chicken, parsley, cooled hazelnuts and diced apple.

Place a lettuce leaf, or more if small, on a slice of bread, top with the chicken salad and another slice of bread. Alternatively, these are delicious (albeit messy) as toasted open sandwiches.

POTATO SALAD WITH CHORIZO CRUMBS

1kg new potatoes, rinsed and
    halved
1 teaspoon olive oil
75g chorizo, cut into small cubes
    the size of large breadcrumbs
25g panko breadcrumbs
4 tablespoons good-quality
    mayonnaise (check the label
    to make sure it's dairy-free)
2 teaspoons lemon juice
2 spring onions (white and green
    parts), finely chopped
Sea salt and freshly ground
    black pepper

Serves 6

This potato salad is inspired by the migas dishes you find all over
Spain – fried breadcrumbs which were once "cooked on little braziers"
by shepherds, according to Claudia Roden. These days they're a
tapas bar staple, fried in olive oil (or sometimes pork fat). Here I've
combined small crumbs of chorizo with crispy panko, which hungrily
soak up the fiery rust-coloured oil from the sausage. They taste
absolutely delicious sprinkled over potato salad.

Add the potatoes to a large pan of boiling, salted water. Return to
the boil, then turn the heat down and simmer for 15–20 minutes until
tender. Drain and leave to cool.

Meanwhile, heat the oil in a small frying pan over a medium-high heat.
Add the chorizo and fry for a couple of minutes before adding the
panko crumbs. Fry for another 3–4 minutes, stirring regularly until the
chorizo and panko are all crispy. Transfer to a plate lined with kitchen
paper and leave to cool slightly.

In a large bowl, toss the potatoes with the mayonnaise, lemon juice
and spring onions. Season and add half the chorizo crumb mixture.
Toss to coat and serve with extra chorizo crumbs sprinkled on top.

Note: To make this dish gluten-free, leave out the panko and add
1 tablespoon sesame seeds to the salad at the same time as the
spring onions.

REUBENS

2 ½ tablespoons sauerkraut
2 slices soft rye bread
3 slices salt beef
Rapeseed oil
Dill pickle, to serve

FOR THE RUSSIAN DRESSING

2 tablespoons good-quality
  mayonnaise (check the label
  to make sure it's dairy-free)
1 teaspoon tomato ketchup
½ teaspoon horseradish sauce
½ teaspoon Worcestershire
  sauce
¼ teaspoon smoked paprika
2 chives, very finely chopped

Serves 1

Reubens are a New York classic. They may be synonymous with Jewish delis but ironically they're not kosher as they usually contain both meat and cheese. I've removed the Swiss cheese but created a DIY Reuben with a smoky Russian dressing that I hope does justice to deli-owner Arnold Reuben's original. You can of course add even more beef to make it a true NYC-style sandwich...

Drain the sauerkraut in a fine-mesh colander by pressing down with a wooden spoon to get rid of any excess water, then pat dry between two pieces of kitchen paper, squeezing to get rid of any more water. For the Russian dressing, whisk together all the ingredients in a small bowl.

Spread a generous amount of the dressing on one slice of the bread. Lay the slices of beef on top and top with the sauerkraut. Spread a thin amount of dressing on the other slice of bread. Spread a little rapeseed oil onto the topside of this slice of bread.

Heat a large, heavy-bottomed frying pan over a medium-high heat. Add the sandwich, oiled side down, and fry for 3–4 minutes until the bread is lightly golden. Meanwhile, carefully spread a little more rapeseed oil on the topside of the other slice of bread. Carefully flip over with a fish slice and fry for a further 2–3 minutes.

Slice in half and serve immediately, with a dill pickle on the side.

KHAO SOI WITH BEEF AND RED PEPPER

2 tablespoons groundnut,
  sunflower or rapeseed oil
410g fresh egg noodles
2 round shallots, diced
1 garlic clove, crushed
2-cm piece of fresh ginger,
  peeled and finely diced
2 tablespoons red Thai curry
  paste
1 teaspoon curry powder
400ml coconut milk
400ml beef stock
1 red pepper, deseeded and
  thinly sliced
2 teaspoons fish sauce
2 teaspoons palm sugar or light
  soft brown sugar
2 thin sirloin steaks (about 250g
  in total), sliced into 5-mm thick
  strips
1 spring onion (white and green
  part), finely sliced
Small handful of fresh coriander,
  roughly chopped
Lime wedges, to serve
Sea salt and freshly ground
  black pepper

Serves 4

Khao soi is a street food dish from Northern Thailand, usually made with chicken or beef. This is a slightly simplified version, given that for true *khao soi* you need to make the paste from scratch. If you can find them, pickled mustard greens are a traditional accompaniment.

Heat the oil in large wok or deep, heavy-bottomed frying pan over a medium-high heat. Slice 50g of the egg noodles into strips 3cm long and fry for 2–3 minutes until crispy. Transfer to a plate lined with kitchen paper and season with salt.

Fry the shallots, garlic and ginger in the same oil (add a little extra if needed) for 2–3 minutes until softened. Add the curry paste and powder and cook for another couple of minutes. Add the coconut milk, stock, red pepper, fish sauce and sugar, stirring well to combine. Bring to the boil, then turn the heat down and simmer for 15 minutes.

Add the rest of the egg noodles to the broth and cook for a further 2 minutes. Turn the heat up a little, add the steak slices and cook until medium rare. Season with salt and pepper.

Divide between bowls and top each with some fried egg noodles, spring onion and coriander. Serve with lime wedges.

LAMB SHOULDER WITH PUY LENTILS, POMEGRANATE AND A WARM MINT DRESSING

2 tablespoons pomegranate
   molasses
1 tablespoon rapeseed oil
2 garlic cloves, crushed, plus
   ½ head of garlic, cloves
   separated but unpeeled
1 boneless half shoulder of lamb,
   about 700g
2 bay leaves
Sea salt and freshly ground
   black pepper

FOR THE LENTILS
250g Puy lentils
2 bay leaves
1 large bunch of fresh mint
   leaves, very finely chopped
1 teaspoon caster sugar
120ml boiling water
1 tablespoon balsamic vinegar
3 tablespoons extra-virgin
   olive oil
Seeds of 1 fresh pomegranate
2 large handfuls of rocket

Serves 4

A guaranteed-to-impress-your-friends dish that is actually a cinch to make. Cover the lamb in a sticky pomegranate molasses glaze and leave it to roast in the oven while you put your feet up.

Preheat the oven to 180°C/350°F/Gas Mark 4.

Whisk the pomegranate molasses, oil and crushed garlic together. Cut small, shallow slits in the lamb, then massage the pomegranate and oil mixture all over the lamb. Season with salt and pepper.

Place the unpeeled garlic cloves and bay leaves in a small-medium roasting tin. Place the lamb on top and roast for 1 hour 5 minutes.

10 minutes before the lamb is due out of the oven, put the lentils and bay leaves in a saucepan and cover with twice the lentils' volume in water. Bring to the boil, then reduce the heat, season and simmer for 15-20 minutes until tender.

Meanwhile, remove the lamb from the oven, cover with foil and allow it to rest for 10 minutes. To make the dressing, put the chopped mint in a jug, add the sugar and boiling water and stir. When the mixture has cooled slightly, add the vinegar and oil and whisk together briskly to combine.

Drain the lentils. Pour over the warm mint dressing, then season and fold in the pomegranate seeds and rocket. Serve with slices of the lamb on top.

DINNER

BROOKLYN-STYLE PEANUT NOODLES WITH TOFU AND SNOW PEAS

125g soba noodles

2 tablespoons vegetable, sunflower or groundnut oil

200g firm tofu, drained and dried (see page 92), then cut into 2cm cubes

100g pak choi, trimmed and chopped into large pieces

100g snow peas or mange tout

4 tablespoons crunchy peanut butter

1 tablespoon soy sauce

½ tablespoon rice vinegar

½ teaspoon Sriracha

Juice of ½ lime, plus an extra squeeze to serve

2 tablespoons water

Few drops of sesame oil

1 spring onion (white and green parts), sliced on the diagonal

2 teaspoons sesame seeds, to garnish

Serves 2

Another of those hot-plate suppers I used to make in New York – no oven required (because who needs a kitchen with amazing restaurants on every block). This healthy noodle dish is a riot of textures (tender soba noodles, the crunch of sesame and peanuts, and delicate fried tofu with its crispy coating), and is adapted from a recipe by Jacquie Berger in the excellent *Edible Brooklyn* cookbook, a celebration of that borough's thriving food culture.

Add the noodles to a saucepan of hot water. Bring to the boil and simmer for 3 minutes until al dente. Drain and rinse with cold water.

Meanwhile, heat the oil in a large, heavy-bottomed frying pan over a medium-high heat. Add the tofu and fry until turning crisp and golden on the outside. Add the pak choi and snow peas or mange tout and stir-fry for another 3 minutes, until the tofu is crisp and the vegetables tender and slightly wilted.

Mix the peanut butter, soy sauce, rice vinegar, Sriracha and lime juice together to form a thick paste. Thin with the water to make a thick sauce.

Add the peanut sauce and sesame oil to the pan and toss with the vegetables and tofu so they are well coated. Divide the drained noodles between two plates and top with the tofu and vegetables. Serve immediately, topped with spring onion and sesame seeds, and a squeeze of lime juice.

CHICKEN PIE

6 skinless, boneless chicken
   thighs
½ onion, diced
2 bay leaves
6 sprigs of fresh thyme
6 peppercorns
1 tablespoon olive oil
160g smoked bacon lardons
1 large leek, trimmed and finely
   sliced
50g dairy-free sunflower spread
50g plain flour, plus extra
   for dusting
300ml chicken stock
100ml white wine
1 teaspoon mustard powder
200ml oat cream
500g ready-made puff pastry
   (NOT the all-butter kind)
1 egg, beaten
Sea salt and freshly ground
   black pepper

Pie dish, approximately
   30 x 25cm (or 24cm
   if round), lightly greased

Serves 4

Cut into the golden flaky crust of this pie and underneath you'll find tender chunks of chicken thighs, smoky bacon, leeks and a rich white-wine sauce. It's what winter nights are begging for... (See photograph on page 68.)

Place the chicken thighs in a large saucepan with the onion, bay leaves, 3 of the thyme sprigs, and the peppercorns. Cover with water and bring to the boil. Turn the heat down, cover and poach at a gentle simmer for 15 minutes, or until the chicken is cooked through. Discard the water and herbs and transfer the chicken to a plate lined with kitchen paper.

Heat the oil in a large saucepan over a medium heat and add the lardons and the leaves from the remaining thyme sprigs. Fry for 3-4 minutes until the lardons are crisp and cooked through. Move to one side of the pan and add the leek. Fry over a low-medium heat for 5-6 minutes, until softened.

Meanwhile, melt the dairy-free spread in a separate saucepan over a low-medium heat, then add the flour, stirring continuously until you have a smooth, golden roux. Pour in the chicken stock, increase the heat until the stock is simmering and keep whisking until it is all incorporated into the roux. Stir in the wine, then the mustard powder and oat cream. Simmer for 2-3 minutes then remove from the heat.

Cut the chicken into large chunks. Pour the sauce into the pan with the lardons and leeks. Add the chicken pieces and stir to combine. Season, pour into the pie dish and leave to cool. Meanwhile, preheat the oven to 200°C/400°F/Gas Mark 6.

Lightly dust a work surface and rolling pin with flour, then roll out the pastry to about 5mm thick. Brush the rim of the pie dish with a little beaten egg. Lift up the pastry using your rolling pin, then drape it over the dish. Trim the edges, leaving 2cm pastry over the sides of the dish, then press down and crimp all the way around the edge with your fingertips. Brush the top of the pie with the rest of the beaten egg, then prick a few holes in the centre of the pastry with a fork.

Bake for 35-40 minutes, until the top is golden.

CURRY NIGHT

1. SAAG/PALAK 'PANEER'

2 ½ tablespoons vegetable oil
200g firm tofu, drained and dried
    (see page 92), then cut into
    2-cm cubes
400g baby leaf spinach
2 round shallots, finely diced
Thumb-sized piece of ginger,
    peeled and finely chopped
1 garlic clove, finely chopped
1 teaspoon ground coriander
½ teaspoon ground cumin
½ teaspoon garam masala
½ teaspoon cayenne pepper
4 tablespoons water
50ml coconut milk
Sea salt

*Serves 2 as a main or 4 as a
side dish*

Saag paneer is made with puréed spinach and cubes of firm, mild paneer cheese. It's also known as *palak paneer* as the dish originates from the Punjab where *palak* means spinach (*saag* can refer to other leafy greens). Either way, it's delicious but no friend of the dairy-free. Luckily, firm tofu is a good substitute for paneer, having a similar texture. Fry it first to get it golden and crisp on the outside.

Heat 2 tablespoons of the oil in a heavy-bottomed frying pan over a medium-high heat. Add the tofu and fry until golden, for about 10 minutes. Transfer the tofu to a plate lined with kitchen paper.

Meanwhile, cook the spinach in a pan of boiling water until wilted, for about 3 minutes. Drain well and then purée in a food processor. Leave to one side.

Return the frying pan that you cooked the tofu in to a medium heat and add the remaining ½ tablespoon of oil. Add the shallots and fry for a few minutes until softened. Add the ginger and garlic and fry for a further 1 minute. Add the ground spices and fry for about 1 minute, stirring with a wooden spoon, just until they have released their fragrance.

Add the puréed spinach and the water. Bring to the boil, then simmer for about 3 minutes. Stir the tofu into the mixture before adding the coconut milk and stirring again. Cook for 2 more minutes until the tofu is piping hot. Add salt to taste and serve immediately.

2. TANDOORI CHICKEN

2 chicken legs (about 270g each)
Good pinch of sea salt
Juice of 1 ½ lemons
100g coconut yogurt
½ tablespoon vegetable oil
2 teaspoons tandoori masala
    powder
½ teaspoon cayenne pepper

Serves 2

Fire-engine red tandoori chicken is a curry-house staple. Marinated in yogurt and tandoori spices, it is then blasted in a tandoor oven. While you won't match the furnace heat of the tandoor, nor the ruby hue at home, you can make this delicious approximation with coconut yogurt and a hot oven.

Use a sharp knife to make two deep cuts down the middle of the top side of the chicken legs (the side with most of the meat on it). Put into a baking dish and sprinkle over the salt. Pour two thirds of the lemon juice over the top and rub into the meat. Set aside for 10 minutes.

Mix together the coconut yogurt, the remaining lemon juice and the oil in a large bowl. Stir in the tandoori masala powder and cayenne pepper to make a smooth paste. Pour any lemon juice from the bottom of the dish with the chicken into the marinade and stir to combine. Pour this over the chicken legs, turning to make sure they are well coated all over. Cover with clingfilm and marinate in the fridge for at least 8 hours or overnight.

When ready to cook, preheat the oven to 230°C/450°F/Gas Mark 8. Transfer the chicken legs to another baking dish, shaking off any excess marinade. Cook for 25 minutes or until the chicken juices run clear. Serve with brown rice and fresh naan breads.

3. CHERRY RAITA

125g coconut yogurt
1 garlic clove, crushed
1 tablespoon lemon juice
50g ripe cherries (about 6),
    pitted and finely sliced
Small handful of fresh mint,
    very finely chopped
Sea salt and freshly ground
    black pepper

Serves 4

A luscious, creamy raita with slivers of cherries and fresh mint…

Whisk the yogurt, crushed garlic and lemon juice together until you have a thick sauce. Fold in the cherry slices and mint. Season to taste.

CONFIT DUCK LEGS WITH CARROT AND ORANGE PUREE

1 tablespoon sea salt
2 duck legs
Small handful of fresh thyme
    sprigs
2 garlic cloves, thinly sliced
About 350g duck fat

FOR THE PUREE
400g carrots, peeled and diced
Finely grated zest of ½ orange
    and 1 tablespoon juice
1 garlic clove, crushed
2 ½ tablespoons extra-virgin
    olive oil
Fresh thyme leaves, to sprinkle
Sea salt and freshly ground
    black pepper

Serves 2

This impressive-looking duck dish is actually a cinch to make. It's inspired by a tapa I ate in Seville of crispy, salty duck with pumpkin purée. At the time, Seville's famous orange trees were in full bloom, which inspired me to recreate the dish with oranges and carrots for a shot of sunshine on the plate.

The night before you want to make the dish, rub the salt all over the duck legs, then scatter some of the thyme and garlic over the base of a shallow baking dish. Place the duck legs in the dish, then scatter the rest of the thyme and garlic on top. Cover and chill overnight.

The next day, preheat the oven to 150°C/300°F/Gas Mark 2. Remove the duck from the fridge and pat dry with kitchen paper, removing some but not all of the salt.

Transfer the garlic and thyme to a medium-sized casserole and nestle the duck legs on top. Melt the duck fat in a saucepan over a low heat and then pour it over the top of the duck legs until they are completely covered. The exact amount will depend on the dimensions of your casserole, but if you find yourself slightly short of duck fat, top it up with vegetable or sunflower oil.

Cover and cook in the oven for 2 ½ hours or until very tender. Remove from the oven. (If not using immediately, the cooled duck confit will keep, covered in the fat, in an airtight container in the fridge for a couple of weeks.)

Turn the oven up to 200°C/400°F/Gas Mark 6. To crisp up the duck legs, remove them from the fat and place in a shallow baking dish, skin side up. Roast for 25 minutes, or until the skin is golden and crispy.

Make the carrot purée 20 minutes before the duck is ready to serve. Steam or boil the carrots in a large saucepan until tender. Drain, reserving 2 tablespoons of the cooking water, then return the carrots to the pan off the heat, adding back the reserved water. Add the orange zest and juice, and the crushed garlic. Stir to combine, then pour in the oil. Blitz with a stick blender until smooth and creamy, then season generously.

Serve each duck leg on top of some purée, and sprinkle thyme leaves over the top. Serve with broccoli and a good bottle of red.

TARATOR CHICKEN IN PARMA HAM WITH WALNUT, GRAPE AND RADICCHIO SALAD

150g walnut pieces
6 skinless, boneless chicken
    breasts
75g white breadcrumbs
1 garlic clove, peeled
Large handful of fresh tarragon
    (about 20g), roughly chopped
Large handful of flat-leaf parsley
    (about 28g), roughly chopped
1 tablespoon red wine vinegar
150ml water
100-130ml extra-virgin olive oil,
    plus extra for drizzling
12 slices Parma ham
Sea salt and freshly ground
    black pepper

FOR THE SALAD
2 tablespoons extra-virgin
    olive oil
2 teaspoons red wine vinegar
1 teaspoon caster sugar
150g red grapes, halved
    lengthways
200g radicchio or red chicory,
    finely shredded (substitute
    white chicory if red is out of
    season)
Small handful of fresh tarragon
    leaves, chopped

Serves 6

Tarator means different things in different Eastern European and Middle Eastern countries, but in Turkey it refers to a thick sauce made with breadcrumbs, walnuts and herbs. I first came across it in Sally Butcher's excellent *Persia in Peckham*, and thought it would make a delicious stuffing for chicken breasts wrapped in Parma ham (that noughties dinner-party staple – so often made with a creamy cheese). The recipe for the *tarator* is adapted from Butcher's.

Toast the walnut pieces in a small, dry frying pan over a medium heat until golden. Keep a careful eye on them as they can burn quickly. Tip onto a plate, leave to cool, then chop. Preheat the oven to 200°C/400°F/Gas Mark 6.

Cut along one side of each chicken breast – almost but not all way through – so it opens out like a book.

Put the breadcrumbs, 100g of the chopped walnuts (reserve the remainder for the salad), garlic, tarragon and parsley in a food processor and whizz to combine. Pour in the vinegar and water. Whizz briefly then, with the processor running, pour in the oil in a very slow, steady trickle until you have a thick but wet paste (coarse, but with a similar consistency to hummus). Remove from the processor and season generously.

Fold the chicken breasts out on a chopping board and place a couple of spoonfuls of the *tarator* inside the middle of one half of the opened chicken breast, spreading it along the inside. Close the other half of the chicken breast on top of the mixture. Wrap each chicken breast in two slices of Parma ham, overlapping each other, with the ends of the ham tucked underneath the chicken breast.

Space the chicken breasts out in a roasting tin and drizzle a little oil over the top. Bake for 25 minutes until the Parma ham is crisp, the chicken is cooked through and its juices run clear.

Meanwhile, to make the salad, whisk the oil, vinegar and sugar together to combine. Toss this dressing with the grape halves, reserved toasted, chopped walnuts, shredded radicchio and most of the tarragon leaves, in a large bowl. Garnish with the rest of the tarragon leaves and divide between serving plates. Serve with the chicken to one side.

DAUPHINOISE POTATOES

25g dairy-free sunflower spread,
plus extra for greasing
650g Desiree potatoes, peeled
200ml almond milk
25g plain flour
1 ½ teaspoons mustard powder
2 large garlic cloves, crushed
250ml oat cream
½ teaspoon ground nutmeg
Sea salt and freshly ground
black pepper

Serves 6

Creamy layers of potatoes drowning in cream and cheese – I must admit, I wasn't optimistic about recreating Dauphinoise potatoes. But, after a couple of trial runs, I've cracked it. The trick is to make a white sauce instead of just adding dairy-free milk and oat cream to the potatoes (they'll split if you do), and to give it a little *umami* kick with mustard powder. Grill it for 5 minutes at the end and the result is a golden Dauphinoise you'll be proud to serve to the most committed dairy-eater.

Preheat the oven to 160°C/320°F/Gas Mark 3. Grease a medium-sized gratin or other ovenproof dish with dairy-free spread. Slice the potatoes (or carefully use a mandolin) into 3-mm slices.

Put the almond milk in a saucepan, season with a little salt and bring to the boil, then turn down to a simmer.

Meanwhile, melt the dairy-free spread in a separate saucepan over a low-medium heat, then add the flour, stirring until you have a smooth roux. Pour the almond milk onto the roux, whisking until all the milk is incorporated. Stir in the mustard powder and garlic and simmer for 2 minutes, before adding the oat cream. Simmer for another 2–3 minutes, then adjust the seasoning and remove from the heat.

Arrange the potato slices in layers in the baking dish. Pour the sauce all over them, making sure the potatoes are well covered in the sauce. Use a small fine-mesh sieve to sprinkle the nutmeg over the top of the potatoes.

Bake on the middle shelf in the oven for 1 hour, until the potatoes are tender. Preheat the grill just before they are ready, then grill for 5 minutes, or until the top has lots of enticing golden patches.

AMERICAN BARBECUE NIGHT

1. 'BUTTERMILK' CHICKEN

1 tablespoon lemon juice
300ml almond milk
2 teaspoons plain soya yogurt
3 teaspoons cayenne pepper
3 teaspoons mustard powder
4 garlic cloves, peeled and
  bashed with the flat of a knife
2 teaspoons sea salt and plenty
  of freshly ground black pepper
2 teaspoons maple syrup
1kg chicken thighs and
  drumsticks
Olive oil

Serves 4

What if you could get the tenderness of fried chicken without all the deep-fried grease? Enter 'buttermilk' roast chicken, adapted from a Nigella Lawson recipe. Thighs and drumsticks (so much more flavoursome than chicken breasts) get a long marinating in garlic, spices and a dairy-free 'buttermilk' – the result is chicken with burnished-gold skin and succulent meat. No deep-frying required. The perfect accompaniments have to be cornbread and slaw (see pages 80-81).

Add the lemon juice to the almond milk, stir, leave to rest for 5 minutes, then stir in the soya yogurt.

To make the marinade, add the cayenne pepper, mustard powder, bashed garlic cloves, salt, pepper and maple syrup to the almond 'buttermilk', whisking briskly with a fork to combine.

Place the chicken thighs and drumsticks in a large, sealable freezer bag. Pour in the marinade, seal and place flat in a baking dish in the fridge, making sure the chicken is well coated. Marinate in the fridge for at least 6 hours or overnight.

Preheat the oven to 220°C/425°F/Gas Mark 7. Remove the chicken from the marinade and shake off any excess liquid. Space the chicken pieces out in a roasting tin, drizzle with a little oil and roast for 30 minutes, until the chicken is cooked through and the skin is golden brown with dark, burnished patches.

2. RED CABBAGE AND SESAME SLAW

50ml lemon juice
50ml white wine vinegar
1 tablespoon caster sugar
1 red cabbage, finely shredded
1 spring onion (white and green
    part), sliced
Large handful of coriander
    leaves
1 tablespoon sesame seeds
Sea salt and freshly ground
    black pepper

Serves 6-8

A peppy slaw to serve at a barbecue, with 'buttermilk' chicken (see page 78) or pulled pork and ribs. Calcium-rich sesame seeds add texture and crunch, while coriander and lemon juice add freshness and zest, meaning there's no need for mayo.

Whisk together the lemon juice, vinegar and sugar. Pour this mixture over the shredded cabbage and stir to combine.

Add the spring onion, coriander and sesame seeds. Season and toss everything together well.

3. DAIRY-FREE CORNBREAD

340ml soya or almond milk
Juice of ½ lemon
200g polenta
40g self-raising flour, sifted
1 teaspoon baking powder
½ teaspoon bicarbonate of soda
50g caster sugar
1 teaspoon sea salt
1 large egg, beaten
30g dairy-free sunflower spread,
    melted and cooled
1 spring onion (white and green
    part), finely sliced

20 x 20cm square baking tin,
    greased and lined

Makes 16 squares/Serves 8

There's something comforting about cornbread. It's that golden crust combined with the soft, primrose-yellow base. This sweet staple of the American South is basically cake you can get away with eating with savoury dishes - serve it with a deep-red, smoky chilli, or with the 'buttermilk' chicken (see page 78) and red cabbage and sesame slaw opposite.

Preheat the oven to 200°C/400°F/Gas Mark 6.

Mix together the soya or almond milk and lemon juice in a measuring jug and leave to stand for 5 minutes.

Meanwhile, fold all the dry ingredients together in a large bowl with a large metal spoon, until just combined. Pour in the almond milk and lemon juice mixture, add the egg, melted spread and spring onion and whisk together to combine.

Pour the batter into the prepared tin and bake for 25 minutes, or until golden on top. Leave to cool for 5 minutes in the tin, before cutting into squares and turning out onto a wire rack to cool slightly. Best served when still warm.

VIETNAMESE CHICKEN AND PUMPKIN CURRY

2 lemongrass stalks, peeled and
  finely sliced
3 garlic cloves, finely chopped
1 tablespoon sunflower or
  vegetable oil
2 round shallots, finely diced
2 tablespoons curry powder
1 teaspoon ground turmeric
450g skinless, boneless chicken
  thighs, diced
400ml chicken stock
250g pumpkin or butternut
  squash, deseeded and cut
  into 2-cm cubes
200g potatoes, peeled and cut
  into 2-cm cubes
250ml coconut milk
3 teaspoons sugar
30ml fish sauce
Fresh coriander leaves,
  to garnish
Red chilli, sliced, to garnish
  (optional)
Sea salt and freshly ground
  black pepper

Serves 4

Vietnamese curry is so creamy and satisfying, it's hard to believe it's not laced with dairy. I developed a minor addiction to it on honeymoon in Vietnam, where the chef at our hotel gave me his recipe after I kept ordering it. After playing around with the dish back home, this is my version – the sweet pumpkin or squash makes a great foil for the umami-rich broth. Vietnamese curry is often served with a crisp baguette, but also works well with white or brown rice.

Blitz the lemongrass and garlic in a small food processor or mini chopper to form a thick paste.

Heat a large, heavy-bottomed saucepan over a medium heat. Add the oil, then fry the shallots for about 4 minutes, until softened. Add the lemongrass and garlic paste and fry for 2 minutes, until fragrant. Stir the curry powder and turmeric into the mixture and fry for just 30 seconds, then add the diced chicken. Fry for a couple of minutes until the chicken is coated in the spices and starting to brown, then pour in the stock.

Bring the stock to the boil, then add the diced pumpkin or squash and the potatoes. Reduce the heat slightly, season, cover and simmer for 10 minutes.

Add the coconut milk, sugar and fish sauce. Simmer, uncovered, over a medium-high heat for another 5 minutes. Check the chicken is cooked through and check the seasoning.

Garnish with the coriander leaves, and slices of red chilli if desired, and serve with lime wedges.

TOAD IN THE HOLE

1 ½ teaspoons fresh thyme
   leaves
250ml soya milk
100g plain flour
1 teaspoon salt
2 large eggs
2 ½ tablespoons vegetable or
   sunflower oil
8 good-quality, herby pork
   sausages (around 450g; and
   (check the label to make sure
   they're dairy-free)

Large roasting tin,
   approx. 35 x 30cm

Serves 4

When I was a kid, toad in the hole was a fixture on my 'top ten dinners' list (as were fishfingers; I was quite the junior gourmand). Even now, there's something about that combination of sausages surrounded by golden, puffy Yorkshire pudding batter that brings back the comforts of a childhood dinner time. My dairy-free twist is to infuse fresh and fragrant thyme leaves in soya milk for 20 minutes before whisking. You'll really notice the difference in the flavour of the batter, and no-one will guess it's made with soya if you don't want them to.

Add the thyme leaves to the soya milk. Stir once and leave to steep for 20 minutes.

Sift the flour and salt into a large bowl. Make a well in the centre and crack in the eggs.

Pour in the thyme-infused soya milk slowly, about one third at a time, whisking after each addition until all the milk is added and the batter is smooth with no lumps. Leave to stand for around 20 minutes. Meanwhile, preheat the oven to 220°C/425°F/Gas Mark 7.

Heat ½ tablespoon of the oil in a large frying pan. Add the sausages and fry until browned all over. Pour the remaining 2 tablespoons of oil into the large roasting tin and place in the hot oven for 5-10 minutes until the oil is smoking.

Remove the tin from the oven and add the sausages, evenly spacing them. Pour in the batter and immediately return to the oven. Cook for 20-25 minutes until the batter is golden and puffed up and the sausages are cooked through. Don't be tempted to open the oven door during cooking as this may cause the batter to sink.

FOR YORKSHIRE PUDDING *Serves 4-6*
Follow the recipe for the batter, as above, but cook in a 12-hole muffin tray, with a little heated oil in each hole and dividing the batter equally between the holes. Bake for 20 minutes, until golden and puffy.

BANGERS AND OLIVE OIL MASH

8 good-quality pork sausages
(check the label to make sure
they're dairy-free)
1kg floury potatoes, such as
Maris Piper, peeled and cubed
4 tablespoons extra-virgin
olive oil
3 tablespoons almond milk
Sea salt and freshly ground
black pepper

Serves 4

Big fluffy clouds of mash don't have to be made with dollops of butter. Olive oil mash is buttery mash's more sophisticated cousin – there's a slight, pleasing hint of extra-virgin that pairs well with most meat dishes, and the mash is every bit as light and creamy as its buttery relative.

Fry, bake or grill the sausages according to your preference.

Place the potatoes in a large pan of cold, salted water. Bring to the boil, then turn the heat down and simmer for about 15 minutes, until tender.

Drain the potatoes and leave in the colander for a few minutes to dry out a bit. Return to the warm pan and pour in the oil. Mash vigorously with a potato masher until lump-free, soft and fluffy. Season, then stir in the almond milk and mash again.

Serve immediately with the sausages. I'm always temped to stick the sausages into a mash mountain, in the manner of *The Beano* comic. Steamed broccoli works as a side dish if you're feeling virtuous (but Dennis the Menace wouldn't approve).

MOJITO SALMON WITH PLANTAIN FRIES

FOR THE SALMON

3 tablespoons stale white
   breadcrumbs or panko
   breadcrumbs
2 teaspoons finely chopped
   mint leaves
Finely grated zest of 1 lime
½ teaspoon sea salt
Good grinding of freshly ground
   black pepper
2 salmon fillets
1 tablespoon olive oil
2 teaspoons rum

FOR THE FRIES

300ml vegetable, sunflower or
   rapeseed oil
1 plantain, still a little green but
   not completely unripe, peeled
   and cut into evenly-sized fries,
   about 7cm long
Sea salt

FOR THE MAYO

Juice of ½ lime
1 teaspoon finely chopped mint
   leaves
1½ teaspoons Sriracha or
   hot sauce
5 tablespoons good-quality
   mayonnaise (check it's
   dairy-free)

Serves 2

In South London, where I lived for many years, the streets are paved with plantains. You'll spot them everywhere, in crates stacked three deep outside West Indian shops. To the untrained eye they look like overgrown bananas, but plantains are much starchier and firmer than their sweeter cousins. For a taste of the tropics on a grey, rainy day, I make this easy dinner of mojito salmon served with plantain fries and a fiery mint and lime mayo. As for the salmon – it's having its own private carnival in the oven with lime, mint and a little rum over crisp breadcrumbs.

Preheat the oven to 190°C/375°F/Gas Mark 5 and line a baking dish with foil or parchment.

Mix together the breadcrumbs, mint, lime zest, salt and pepper on a plate and press the salmon flesh side down into the mixture. Turn the fillets back the right way and place in the baking dish. Sprinkle any remaining breadcrumb mix from the plate over the fillets so they have an even-ish topping of crumbs.

Warm the olive oil in a small frying pan over a medium heat. Remove the pan from the heat (vital if you'd like your eyebrows to remain where they are) and pour in the rum. Return to the heat and melt until the oil and rum are starting to bubble and turn a light golden brown.

Pour the rum mix over the salmon fillets, put in the oven and bake for about 10-12 minutes until the salmon is just cooked through. Turn the grill to high and then grill for about 2 minutes, or until the topping is crisp and golden.

Meanwhile, heat the vegetable oil for the fries in a large, heavy-bottomed frying pan. Once the oil is very hot and starting to smoke, add the plantain and fry for about 3-4 minutes, or until golden brown and tender in the middle. Do this in two batches if necessary, so as not to overcrowd the pan. Take off the heat and transfer the fries with a slotted spoon or kitchen tongs to a plate lined with a few sheets of kitchen paper to absorb the excess oil. Season with salt.

To make the mayo, put all the ingredients into a bowl and whisk briskly with a fork to combine. Check the seasoning and add a little more Sriracha or hot sauce if required. Serve the salmon with the plantain fries, and a simple watercress salad, if desired.

GRIDDLED LAMB STEAKS WITH CIDER GRAVY AND CANNELLINI BEAN AND HERB MASH

2 lamb steaks (about 150g each) or 4 small lamb leg steaks
1 tablespoon vegetable or olive oil
300ml medium-dry cider
1 tablespoon soy sauce
1 ½ tablespoons cornflour
2 ½ tablespoons cold water
Sea salt and freshly ground black pepper

FOR THE BEANS
90g dried cannellini beans
700ml cold water
½ teaspoon bicarbonate of soda
1 ½ tablespoons olive oil
1 garlic clove, crushed
Needles from 2 sprigs of fresh rosemary
Leaves from 3 sprigs of fresh thyme

Serves 2

I love chops, but you don't exactly get a lot of juicy, delicious lamb for your buck. For around the same price, you can pick up a pair of lamb steaks: all meat, no bones. Here I've paired them with cannellini bean and rosemary mash, a traditional Tuscan dish. If you're in a hurry, use a tin of cannellini beans instead, but patience pays off – dried ones soaked overnight make a much softer, creamier mash. Apples and cider are best-known for partnering up with pork, but they also make a delicious compadre for lamb. Though, obviously, this gravy will work really well with pork chops or sausages, too.

Place the cannellini beans in a large bowl, cover with the water, add the bicarbonate of soda and stir to dissolve. Leave to soak overnight or for a minimum of 6 hours.

Drain and rinse the beans. Place in a large, heavy-bottomed saucepan and cover with 700ml cold water. Bring to the boil and boil rapidly for 10 minutes. Turn the heat down, cover and simmer for about 1 hour 20 minutes or until soft and tender. Check the beans regularly, adding more water if necessary. Drain and set aside while you cook the lamb.

Brush both sides of the lamb steaks with a little oil and season with salt and pepper. Heat a griddle or heavy-bottomed frying pan to high and fry for around 3–4 minutes on each side, depending on the thickness of the steaks and how pink you like them. After frying the first side, use kitchen tongs to brown the fat on the side of each steak. Transfer the steaks to two dinner plates and cover with foil to keep them warm.

Heat the oil for the beans in a saucepan over a medium heat and fry the garlic and herbs for 2 minutes. Add the drained beans and heat until piping hot, 1–2 minutes, stirring with a wooden spoon and using it to crush and gently mash the beans, which should still retain some texture. Season liberally with salt and divide between the two plates.

Return the lamb pan to the heat. Pour in the cider and swirl to deglaze the pan. If you used a griddle, decant the mixture into another saucepan. Add the soy sauce, bring to the boil and simmer for 2–3 minutes. Mix the cornflour and water together, then stir into the gravy. Cook for 3–4 minutes, stirring constantly. Pour over the lamb and serve with broccoli, Savoy cabbage or spring greens.

CHORIZO, CANNELLINI BEAN AND ROCKET STIR-FRY

½ tablespoon olive oil
1 red chilli, deseeded and finely
   diced
2 spring onions, finely sliced and
   separated into white and green
   slices
1 x 110g chorizo, cut into 1-cm
   slices
410g tin cannellini beans, rinsed
   and drained
1½ tablespoons balsamic
   vinegar
70g rocket
Sourdough bread, sliced, to serve

*Serves 2 as a light lunch
or supper*

Who says stir-fries have to have Asian ingredients? This Spanish-ish dish is one of my absolute favourite standbys on those nights when you're late back from work and just want some comfort food in a bowl in front of Netflix. It also makes a delicious lunchbox the next day and can be easily doubled.

Heat the oil in a large, heavy-bottomed frying pan over a medium-high heat. Add the chilli and white slices of spring onion and sizzle for about 1 minute.

Add the chorizo and turn the heat up to high. Fry for about 3 minutes or until cooked through and turning crispy around the edges.

Stir in the cannellini beans and cover in all those lovely orange oils released from the chorizo. Stir-fry for around 2 minutes. Pour in the balsamic vinegar and add the rocket. Stir for around 20 seconds, just until slightly wilted.

Top with the green spring onion slices and serve immediately with some sourdough bread.

PRAWN RISOTTO

2 tablespoons olive oil
1 onion, finely diced
2 garlic cloves, crushed
2 sticks of celery, trimmed and
    very finely sliced
280g Arborio risotto rice
225ml dry white wine
750ml hot fish (or chicken) stock
180g raw king prawns
150g frozen peas
1 spring onion (white and green
    part), finely sliced on the
    diagonal
Finely grated zest of ½ lemon
1½ teaspoons finely chopped
    mint
Swirl of extra-virgin olive oil
Sea salt and freshly ground
    black pepper

Serves 4

Don't be wary about making risotto - it's not complicated, just
methodical. There's something meditative about standing at the stove,
stirring with your wooden spoon, while the grains of rice grow fat on
wine and stock. The reward for your patience is a creamy risotto with
plump prawns and the zesty, sunny flavours of peas, mint and lemon...

Heat the oil in a deep, heavy-bottomed saucepan or flameproof
casserole over a low-medium heat. Fry the onion, garlic and celery
gently for 10 minutes until softened. Turn the heat up a little, add the
rice and stir to coat in the oil and vegetables. Fry for 1 minute, then
pour in the wine and simmer for 1 minute.

Turn the heat down to low-medium again and add a ladleful of stock.
Stir with a wooden spoon until the rice has absorbed the stock.
Repeat, adding a ladleful at a time and stirring, while it absorbs, until
you have added all the stock and the rice grains are plump and tender.
Season generously.

Stir in the prawns and peas and cook for 2 minutes, then cover and
cook for a further 2 minutes until the prawns are cooked through.
Stir in the spring onion, most of the lemon zest and 1 teaspoon of
the mint, add the extra-virgin olive oil, then remove from the heat
and leave to sit with the lid on for a couple of minutes. Check the
seasoning, garnish with the remaining mint and lemon zest, and serve.

SALT AND PEPPER TOFU

400g firm tofu
125g cornflour
½ tablespoon sea salt
150ml groundnut, vegetable
    or sunflower oil, plus
    ½ tablespoon
2 garlic cloves, finely sliced
1 red chilli, deseeded and diced
1-2 spring onions (white and
    green parts), sliced
Soy sauce, for drizzling
Freshly ground black pepper

*Serves 2 as a main or 4 as a
starter*

Salt and pepper tofu is one of *those* dishes – if it's on the menu, I have to order it. It's something about the combination of the delicate, mild tofu inside and the crunchy, peppery coating – not to mention all those chillies and garlic. It's easy to make at home, too – just allow plenty of time to drain the tofu before you start frying.

Drain the tofu an hour or so ahead of time by wrapping it in kitchen paper, then in a clean tea towel. Put it in a colander in the sink, then place a heavy object on top and leave to drain. Pat dry and cut into 3-cm cubes.

Combine the cornflour, salt and plenty of black pepper in a large bowl. Add the tofu and toss gently to coat.

Heat the 150ml oil in a large, heavy-bottomed frying pan over a high heat until sizzling. Test whether the oil is hot enough by adding one tofu cube – it should start sizzling straight away. Working in batches, fry the tofu on one side for a couple of minutes until golden, then use kitchen tongs to carefully turn on its sides to brown all over. Transfer to a plate lined with kitchen paper.

Meanwhile, heat the remaining ½ tablespoon oil in a small frying pan over a medium-high heat. Fry the garlic and chilli for 1-2 minutes until the garlic starts to colour. Throw the tofu cubes back in the pan briefly with the spring onion and toss to mix. Arrange on the plates and drizzle soy sauce over the top to serve.

Serve on its own as a starter, or as a main course with rice and Tenderstem broccoli, stir-fried with soy and garlic.

CREAMY SWEET POTATO, BACON
AND THYME PASTA

400g dried orecchiette or
   conchiglie pasta
2 tablespoons olive oil
300g sweet potato, cut into
   2-cm cubes
80g bacon lardons
1 garlic clove, crushed
½ teaspoon ground nutmeg
Leaves from 2 sprigs of fresh
   thyme
150ml oat cream
Small handful of flat-leaf parsley,
   chopped
Sea salt and freshly ground
   black pepper

Serves 4

Creamy pasta needn't belong on your banned list. Make this easy and filling pasta with sweet potato, crisp cubes of bacon and fresh herbs one of your weeknight staples...

Cook the pasta in a pan of salted, boiling water until al dente. Drain, reserving 2 tablespoons of the cooking water.

Meanwhile, heat the oil in a large, heavy-bottomed frying pan over a medium-high heat and fry the sweet potato for 5 minutes until starting to turn golden. Add the lardons and fry for another 1-2 minutes before adding the garlic, nutmeg and thyme. Fry for a further minute, then remove from the heat.

Return the pasta to its pan with the contents of the frying pan. Pour in the oat cream and stir to coat the pasta. Season and add a little of the reserved cooking water to thin the sauce.

Stir in the parsley and serve immediately.

PANCETTA, COURGETTE AND TOMATO CARBONARA

1 tablespoon olive oil
2 garlic cloves, crushed
200g cubetti de pancetta
1 large courgette (about 300g),
 cut into 1-cm cubes
500g dried spaghetti
3 eggs, plus 1 egg yolk
300g medium vine tomatoes,
 halved, deseeded and cut into
 1-cm cubes
Sea salt and freshly ground
 black pepper

Serves 4 (very hungry people)

The idea for this comes from a restaurant somewhere in the back streets of Rome. I can't remember the restaurant's name (it's somewhere in Trastevere and the decor is a bit garish), but I'll never forget their sublime carbonara, studded with garlicky courgettes and tender tomatoes. I first ate it in my pre-dairy-free days, but luckily a bit of a tinker around proves it's just as delicious without mountains of Parmesan.

Heat the oil in a frying pan over a medium heat. Add the garlic and cook for 1-2 minutes before adding the pancetta. Fry for 3-4 minutes until starting to crisp up, before adding the diced courgette. Cook for another 3 minutes until the courgette cubes are tender, then remove from the heat.

Meanwhile, cook the spaghetti in a pan of boiling, well-salted water, until al dente. Beat the eggs and yolk together in a bowl, season generously with black pepper and place to one side.

When the spaghetti is cooked, remove 2 tablespoons of the cooking water and place to one side in a small cup or mug. Drain the rest of the pasta and return to the pan. Add the courgettes, pancetta and oil from the frying pan and toss well, then stir in the diced tomatoes.

Remove from the heat and pour in the beaten eggs, stirring quickly as you do so to coat all the spaghetti strands. Add the reserved cooking water, a little at a time and only if needed, to loosen the sauce slightly. Season with salt and more pepper, to taste. Eat straight away.

FISH PIE

**FOR THE MASHED
POTATO TOPPING**

1kg floury potatoes, such as
  Maris Piper, cubed
4 tablespoons light olive oil
3 tablespoons almond milk
2 teaspoons panko breadcrumbs
  (optional)
Sea salt and freshly ground
  black pepper

FOR THE FILLING

½ onion, finely chopped
1 bay leaf
6 black peppercorns
2 cloves
640g fresh fish fillets, a mixture
  of sustainably-sourced smoked
  haddock, salmon and white
  fish, such as pollack, deboned,
  skinned and diced
500ml soya or almond milk
100g raw, peeled king prawns
50g dairy-free sunflower spread
50g plain flour
2 teaspoons mustard powder
250ml oat cream
Small handful of flat-leaf parsley,
  finely chopped

Baking dish, approximately
  28 x 22cm

Serves 4-6

Fish pie is a duvet of a dinner – so cosy and warming you just want to burrow into it. No wonder it never really goes out of fashion. This version is every bit as good as milk-laden versions: a rich, creamy sauce, tender flaked fish, and a layer of fluffy mash on top.

Place the potatoes in a large pan of cold, salted water. Bring to the boil, then turn the heat down and simmer for around 15 minutes until tender. Drain and leave in the colander for a few minutes to dry out a bit, then return them to the warm pan and pour in the oil. Mash vigorously with a potato masher until lump-free, soft and fluffy. Season, then stir in the almond milk and mash again.

Preheat the oven to 200°C/400°F/Gas Mark 6.

Meanwhile, put the onion, bay leaf, peppercorns, cloves and fish (not the prawns) into a large pan and pour in the soya or almond milk. Bring to a gentle boil, then poach the fish at a gentle simmer for 5 minutes. Add the prawns and continue to simmer for another 2–3 minutes, until the fish and prawns are cooked through.

Using a fish slice, transfer the fish, prawns and onions to the baking dish, making a layer of fish on the bottom of the dish. Set the infused milk to one side.

Melt the dairy-free spread in a clean pan over a low-medium heat, then add the flour, stirring continuously until you have a smooth roux. Place a sieve above the roux and strain the milk mixture through it, discarding the bay and spices. Whisk until all the milk is incorporated into the roux. Stir in the mustard powder, before adding the oat cream. Simmer for another 2–3 minutes then remove from the heat, add salt and pepper to taste, stir in the chopped parsley and then pour over the fish.

Top with the mashed potato, using a fork to fluff the top. Sprinkle the panko breadcrumbs over the top, if using, and bake for 30–35 minutes until the peaks of the mashed potato, and the breadcrumbs if using, are golden. Serve immediately.

TOASTED WALNUT PESTO

70g walnut pieces
30g cashew nuts, chopped into
   small pieces
1 small garlic clove, peeled
Bunch of flat-leaf parsley (28g)
Bunch of basil (28g)
110ml extra-virgin olive oil
Sea salt

Makes 1 jar

This versatile pesto tastes great tossed through pasta and gnocchi or on top of baked chicken and fish. The creamy cashews temper the earthy flavour of the walnuts and mean there's no need for Parmesan.

Toast the walnuts in a dry frying pan over a medium heat until they start turning golden. Keep a careful eye on them – they can go from golden to charred in a matter of seconds. Transfer to a plate and allow them to cool completely.

Once the walnuts are cooled, roughly chop them and tip into a food processor, along with the cashews, garlic, parsley, basil and oil. Blitz until you have the desired consistency.

Season with salt to taste. If not using immediately, spoon the pesto into a clean jar, cover the top with extra-virgin olive oil and refrigerate for up to 1 week.

PORK, LEMONGRASS
AND MINT MEATBALLS

½ tablespoon olive oil
2 round shallots, finely diced
1 green chilli, halved and
    deseeded
1 lemongrass stalk (white part
    only), cut into thin slices
1 small handful of mint leaves
500g lean pork mince
1 egg
75g panko breadcrumbs
Pinch of sea salt and freshly
    ground black pepper

FOR THE SAUCE
2 tablespoons brown sugar
4 tablespoons water
2 tablespoons soy sauce
2 tablespoons mirin
2 tablespoons lemon juice
1 lemongrass stalk (white part
    only), cut into very thin slices

Serves 4

These fluffy pork meatballs are served with a light sauce (more of a drizzle), which enhances, rather than detracts from, the peppy Thai flavours of lemongrass and mint. As long as you've got time to chill them in the fridge before baking, they make a quick and easy mid-week dinner.

Heat the oil in a small frying pan over a medium heat and fry the shallots for 3-4 minutes until softened. Transfer to a plate and leave to cool.

Put the chilli, lemongrass and mint leaves in a small food processor and whizz until they form a paste. Scrape into a large bowl with the pork mince, cooled shallots, egg and panko breadcrumbs. Season, then mix together with your hands until all the ingredients are well incorporated.

Form 50-g balls from the mixture by rolling and pressing between your palms - the mixture should make 12 balls. Arrange on a baking tray lined with baking parchment and chill in the fridge for 30 minutes-1 hour. Preheat the oven to 210°C/425°F/Gas Mark 7.

Bake the chilled meatballs for 16-18 minutes, turning the tray once or twice so all the balls cook evenly, until golden on the outside and cooked through.

Meanwhile, make the sauce by heating the sugar and water in a small pan over a medium-high heat. Bring to the boil, then turn down the heat slightly and stir with a wooden spoon until all the sugar has dissolved. Add the soy, mirin, lemon juice and lemongrass and simmer for 5 minutes until reduced slightly. Strain through a small strainer into a small jug (to remove the lemongrass pieces) to drizzle over the meatballs or serve on the side.

Serve with rice and wilted Asian greens, such as pak choi.

CHEESE-FREE MARGHERITA PIZZA

FOR THE BASE

500g strong white flour,
    ideally '00', plus extra for
    dusting
7-g sachet fast-action dried yeast
300ml warm water
1 teaspoon sea salt
1 tablespoon olive oil

**FOR THE SAUCE AND
TOPPING**

400g good-quality, tinned
    whole tomatoes
½ teaspoon caster sugar
½ tablespoon extra-virgin
    olive oil
A little olive oil, for frying
125g basil tofu, thinly sliced then
    cut into small pieces
Basil leaves, to sprinkle
Sea salt and freshly ground
    black pepper

Makes 4

Don't tell the purists, but I've added basil tofu to this pizza instead of cheese – lightly fried first to give it a golden deliciousness. To recreate a blisteringly hot pizza oven at home, take a tip from the brilliant Pizza Pilgrims in London: use a frying pan. Trust me, it works!

Sieve the flour into a large bowl and make a well in the centre. Mix the yeast in the warm water until dissolved, then slowly pour into the well, working it into the mixture with a wooden spoon and then, once the mixture starts coming together, with your hands. Add the salt. Bring the dough together into a ball, and knead vigorously on a lightly floured surface for 10-15 minutes, until nicely elastic. (Hold a portion of dough up to the light and stretch gently – if it tears it needs more kneading, and if it stretches so it is almost translucent, it's ready.)

Grease a large bowl with the oil and add the dough, turning to make sure it is well oiled. Cover with clingfilm and leave for 1 hour in a warm place until doubled in size. Meanwhile, make the sauce. Put the tomatoes in a pan over a medium heat and crush gently with a spoon. Add the sugar and simmer for 10 minutes, until thickened. Stir in the extra-virgin olive oil. Season, then remove from the heat.

Turn the risen dough out onto a floured surface and knock back with the heel of your hand. Divide into 4 balls. Wrap 3 in clingfilm and set aside in a cool place. Press the remaining dough ball down with your fingertips to create a disc. Place your palms at opposite sides of the disc and gently push them outwards to stretch the dough further, rotating it as you go. (If this is tricky, use a rolling pin, gently.) Once the dough is side-plate-sized, pick it up and drape over the knuckles of both hands. Gently pull your hands apart to stretch the dough, rotating it as you go. Do this until it is thin and dinner-plate-sized, but thicker around the edges. Repeat with the remaining dough balls.

Heat a little olive oil in a small frying pan over a medium heat. Fry the tofu for a couple of minutes, until starting to turn golden. Remove from the heat. Preheat the grill to maximum. Heat a large, heavy-bottomed, ovenproof frying pan over a very high heat. Add a pizza base to the pan, spread a little tomato sauce onto it, leaving a 2-cm border, and cook for 2-3 minutes depending on the strength of your grill, until the edges start to puff up and the bottom has patches of char. Spread a quarter of the tofu on the sauce, sprinkle with basil and grill in the pan for 2-3 minutes, or until cooked through. Repeat to cook all 4 pizzas.

LASAGNE

FOR THE RAGU

1 tablespoon olive oil
1 onion, finely chopped
2 garlic cloves, finely chopped
2 sticks of celery, finely sliced
500g steak mince
400g tin chopped tomatoes
1 tablespoon tomato purée
125ml red wine
Small handful of flat-leaf parsley,
    chopped
Sea salt and freshly ground
    black pepper

FOR THE BÉCHAMEL SAUCE
AND PASTA

500ml almond milk
1 small onion, finely chopped
1 bay leaf
6 black peppercorns
2 cloves
50g dairy-free sunflower spread,
    plus extra for greasing
50g plain flour
1 tablespoon mustard powder
170ml oat cream
About 9 lasagne sheets (the no
    pre-cook kind)
½ teaspoon ground nutmeg
2 tablespoons panko
    breadcrumbs

Deep baking dish, approximately
    28 x 22cm, greased

Serves 6

A lovingly-cooked lasagne is a beautiful thing: creamy béchamel, rich ragu and layers of tender pasta. With this much going on there's no need to smother it in cheese. A dusting of panko crumbs adds a golden crunch to the topping, and a smidgen of mustard powder apes the bite of Parmesan.

For the ragu, heat the oil in a large, heavy-bottomed frying pan over a medium heat. Cook the onion for 5-10 minutes until softened. Stir in the garlic and celery and cook for a further 3 minutes. Add the steak mince and cook, stirring, for around 4 minutes until browned.

Turn the heat up to medium-high and stir in the chopped tomatoes, tomato purée, wine and parsley. Season and simmer over a low heat, uncovered, for 1 hour.

Meanwhile, make the béchamel. Pour the almond milk into a saucepan and stir in the onion, bay leaf, peppercorns and cloves. Season with a little salt and bring to the boil, then lower the heat and simmer for 10 minutes (don't worry if the sauce splits a little at this stage) before removing from the heat and leaving to infuse until needed. Preheat the oven to 200°C/400°F/Gas Mark 6.

When the ragu is almost ready, melt the dairy-free spread in a separate saucepan over a low-medium heat, then add the flour, stirring until you have a smooth roux. Place a sieve above the roux and strain the infused almond milk through it, discarding the onion, bay leaf and spices (although I like to add some of the onions to the ragu at this stage, rather than wasting them all). Whisk until all the milk is incorporated into the roux, then stir in the mustard powder and simmer for 2 minutes, before adding the oat cream. Simmer for another 2-3 minutes, then remove from the heat.

Spread about one third of the ragu over the bottom of the baking dish and arrange a layer of the lasagne sheets on top, and then a quarter of the béchamel. Repeat until you have three layers of pasta and a thicker layer of béchamel on top.

Sprinkle the nutmeg and panko breadcrumbs over the top and bake for around 30 minutes until the top is bubbling and the panko crumbs are golden.

STICKY LIME AND SOY CHICKEN WITH NEW POTATOES, PARSNIPS AND SHALLOTS

600g new potatoes, halved
1-2 parsnips, cut into large pieces
2 tablespoons vegetable,
    sunflower or rapeseed oil, plus
    2 teaspoons for the glaze
2 tablespoons lime marmalade
2 ½ teaspoons soy sauce
1 garlic clove, crushed
6 small round shallots, peeled
    and halved
4 large chicken legs, skin on
Sea salt and freshly ground
    black pepper

Serves 4

This is one of those nifty, one-pan chicken dishes just made for busy nights. Think of it as a mini roast, without the faff. Sticky lime and soy-glazed chicken legs sit happily roasting on a bed of golden potatoes and parsnips while you get on with your evening, and even the pan juices make a delicious 'instant' sauce.

Preheat the oven to 200°C/400°F/Gas Mark 6.

Toss the potatoes and parsnips with the 2 tablespoons oil. Season, place in a large roasting tin and roast for 15 minutes.

Mix the lime marmalade, soy sauce, garlic and the 2 teaspoons oil together to make a glaze. Add the shallots to the roasting tin, tossing with the potatoes and parsnips. Arrange the chicken legs on top of the vegetables, then brush the tops generously with the sticky lime glaze.

Roast for 50-55 minutes or until the chicken is dark gold and the juices running clear, and the vegetables are tender. Serve with French beans and the sauce from the pan.

BEEF SHIN AND CRAFT ALE STEW WITH CRISPY-SAGE DUMPLINGS

FOR THE STEW

30g plain flour
700g beef shin, trimmed and
    diced
3 tablespoons olive oil
1 onion, diced
2 sticks of celery, trimmed and
    thickly sliced
2 bay leaves
2 sprigs of thyme
300ml beef stock
275ml dark craft ale or porter,
    such as Fuller's London Porter
3 large carrots, chopped into
    large chunks
Sea salt and freshly ground
    black pepper

FOR THE DUMPLINGS

1 teaspoon olive oil
Small handful of fresh sage
    leaves, finely shredded
75g suet
150g self-raising flour

Serves 4

A classic beef stew to bring comfort on chilly nights. Choose a rich and chocolatey craft ale for the sauce, such as porter, a traditional beer similar to stout. It was named for the river porters in London who used to have it daily with oysters. Porter is having something of a renaissance and is easy to find in off-licences and supermarkets.

Spread the flour onto a plate and season with salt and pepper. Dredge the diced beef in the seasoned flour to coat.

Heat 2 tablespoons of the oil in a large flameproof casserole over a medium heat. Fry the beef for about 2 minutes on each side, until browned all over, working in several batches so as not to crowd the pan, and adding a little more oil if necessary. Transfer the browned beef to a plate using kitchen tongs or a slotted spoon.

Add the remaining tablespoon of oil to the pan and gently fry the onion for 3–4 minutes. Add the celery, bay leaves and thyme sprigs and cook for another 5 minutes until the vegetables are softened and starting to colour. Stir in a little of the stock and deglaze the bottom of the pan. Tip in the rest of the stock, the ale and the beef, and any remaining flour from the plate. Bring to the boil, then turn the heat down, cover and simmer for 2 hours. Add the carrots, top up with a dash more ale if needed and simmer for another 20 minutes.

Meanwhile, preheat the oven to 180°C/350°F/Gas Mark 4. Heat the oil for the dumplings in a small frying pan over a medium heat. Fry the shredded sage leaves until crispy, then transfer to a plate lined with kitchen paper and leave to cool. Once cool, finely chop.

Rub the suet into the flour in a bowl with your fingertips until it resembles coarse breadcrumbs. Mix in the crispy sage and season with salt. Add just enough cold water, 1 teaspoon at a time, to bring the mixture together into a dough. Roll into small golf-ball-sized balls and place on top of the stew (the bottoms should be in the liquid and the top halves exposed). Transfer the casserole to the oven, uncovered, and cook for another 25–30 minutes, or until the dumplings are cooked through and golden and crisp on top.

Serve with olive oil mash (see page 85) and spring greens. A glass of the craft ale wouldn't go amiss, either.

PURPLE SPROUTING BROCCOLI WITH LEMON, GARLIC AND TOASTED ALMONDS

1 tablespoon flaked almonds
200g purple sprouting broccoli
   (or tenderstem if PSB isn't in
   season), ends trimmed
1 tablespoon extra-virgin olive oil
2 garlic cloves, finely sliced
Finely grated zest and juice of
   ½ lemon
Sea salt

Serves 4-6 as a side dish

Purple sprouting broccoli, with its delicate flavour and gorgeous violet florets, is one of the culinary treasures of early spring. It pairs well with strong flavours like garlic, enhanced here by some fresh lemon and a sprinkling of toasted almonds. Delicious with both roast lamb and chicken.

Toast the flaked almonds in a small, dry frying pan over a medium-high heat until golden - keep a careful eye on them as they can burn quickly. Remove from the heat and tip onto a plate.

Lightly cook the purple sprouting broccoli in a pan of boiling water for 5-6 minutes until just tender, then drain and return to the warm pan.

Meanwhile, heat the oil in a small frying pan (use the same one that you toasted the almonds in) over a medium-high heat, and fry the garlic for 1-2 minutes, until it starts to colour but not burn. Add the lemon juice and stir.

Pour this mixture over the broccoli and toss to coat. Sprinkle with the toasted almonds, the lemon zest and a little salt, and serve immediately.

CARAMELISED CHANTENAY CARROTS

500g Chantenay or baby carrots, topped
2 teaspoons golden caster sugar
1 tablespoon coconut oil
2 tablespoons water
Sea salt and freshly ground black pepper
Fresh coriander, finely chopped, and sesame seeds, or flat-leaf parsley, chopped (see recipe)

Serves 4

These sticky, tender baby carrots are a doddle to make and a versatile side dish. To serve with Asian dishes or at barbecues, toss the carrots with sesame seeds and coriander. To serve with a roast, sprinkle with flat-leaf parsley.

Boil the carrots for about 8-10 minutes in a large pan of lightly salted water, until just tender. Drain and return to the pan. Turn the heat down to medium and add the sugar, coconut oil and water.

Stir to coat all the carrots and simmer for 10-15 minutes, stirring occasionally, until the carrots are caramelised in patches.

Remove from the heat, season and toss with either coriander and sesame seeds or flat-leaf parsley.

DESSERT

COCONUT CUSTARD TARTS

2 tablespoons icing sugar
500g block of ready-made
   puff pastry (NOT the
   all-butter kind)
4 egg yolks
2 tablespoons golden
   caster sugar
2 teaspoons cornflour
400ml coconut milk
2 teaspoons vanilla extract
½ teaspoon ground cinnamon

12-hole muffin tray, generously
   greased with dairy-free spread

Makes 12

Portuguese custard tarts (*pastéis de nata*), are one of life's greatest little pleasures. But since going dairy-free I've had to stare longingly at them through bakery windows...Until I stopped moping and made my own. I've taken a tip from baking guru Richard Bertinet here, and dusted the worktop with icing sugar – it really gives the pastry a sweet edge.

Lightly dust your work surface with the icing sugar and roll out the puff pastry block to a thickness of around 5mm. Cut out 12 circles using a 10-cm round cookie cutter. Press these into the holes of the prepared muffin tray. Prick the bottoms of each case lightly with a fork then put the tray in the fridge to chill while you make the coconut custard. Preheat the oven to 200°C/400°F/Gas Mark 6.

Whisk the egg yolks, sugar and cornflour together in a bowl. Pour the coconut milk into a saucepan and stir in the vanilla extract. Heat until simmering over a low-medium heat, removing it just when it starts to bubble around the edges of the pan; don't let it boil.

Pour onto the egg and sugar mixture in a slow, steady stream, whisking constantly with a balloon whisk to combine. Once you've got a smooth custard, return it to the pan and cook over a very low heat, stirring with a wooden spoon, until quite thick.

Remove the muffin tray from the fridge and pour the custard into the 12 pastry cases. Use a small, fine-mesh sieve to sprinkle a little cinnamon over the tops of the custards. Bake on a high shelf in the oven for 25 minutes, or until the pastry is golden and the custard is set.

Remove from the oven and leave to cool for 2 minutes in the tin before transferring the tarts to a wire rack to cool. To get the tarts out of the tin, use a dinner knife to go round the edges of each half, then twist to lift up the bottom (and don't worry if a few flakes of pastry fall away or stay behind, it won't impact on the tarts' deliciousness). Best eaten when still slightly warm.

RASPBERRY TRIFLE

25ml sherry
1 tablespoon icing sugar
220g fresh raspberries
Double quantity of whipped
    coconut cream (see page 137)
Toasted flaked almonds,
    to decorate

FOR THE TRIFLE SPONGES
(Makes around 20)
2 eggs, separated
70g golden caster sugar
½ teaspooon vanilla extract
70g plain flour, sifted
Icing sugar, for dusting

FOR THE COCONUT CUSTARD
5 egg yolks
75g golden caster sugar
2 tsp cornflour
300ml coconut milk
200ml coconut cream
Seeds of 1 vanilla pod or
    ½ teaspoon vanilla powder
    (optional)
2 teaspoons vanilla extract

Piping bag, fitted with a plain
    2-cm nozzle, or a disposable
    bag with the end snipped off
    to the right width

Serves 8

Trifle is normally a dairy festival in a glass bowl. Thanks to our trusty friends, coconut milk and cream, you can make this delicious milk-free version (it even won thumbs up from my dad, an ardent trifle fan). Most shop-bought trifle sponges contain milk powder, but homemade ones are pretty simple to make. I've adapted the trifle sponges recipe from one for Naples biscuits by the food writer Mary-Anne Boermans.

To make the trifle sponges, preheat the oven to 200°C/400°F/Gas Mark 6 and grease and line 2 baking trays. Whisk the egg whites using an electric whisk, adding half of the sugar a little at a time, and whisk after each addition until you have stiff peaks.

Use the electric whisk to beat the egg yolks, the vanilla extract and the remaining sugar together, until pale and creamy – this will take about 5 minutes, so keep going until you get the desired consistency. Gently fold the whisked whites into the yolk mixture using a large metal spoon, then gently fold in the flour just until combined. Fill the piping bag with the mixture then pipe 7cm-long biscuits onto the baking tray, spacing them well apart. Bake for 10-15 minutes until lightly golden and crisp. Leave to cool, then dust with icing sugar.

Whisk the egg yolks for the custard in a bowl with the sugar and cornflour. Pour the coconut milk and cream into a saucepan and stir in the vanilla seeds or powder if using, and the vanilla extract. Heat until simmering over a low-medium heat, removing it just when it starts to bubble around the edges of the pan; don't let it boil. Pour onto the egg and sugar mixture in a slow, steady stream, whisking constantly with a balloon whisk. Once smooth, return it to the pan and cook over a very low heat, stirring with a wooden spoon, until it is quite thick – be patient and don't turn the heat up; it **will** thicken. Leave to cool.

To assemble, arrange the trifle sponges in the bottom of a large glass or trifle bowl so you have a snug layer. You may not need all of them. Pour the sherry on the sponges. In a large bowl, mix the icing sugar and half the raspberries, crushing the berries lightly with a fork to release some of their juices, but still retaining some shape. Layer the crushed raspberries on top of the trifle sponges, then top with the remaining raspberries. Pour the cooled custard over the top and smooth it so you have a flat layer. Refrigerate for 30 minutes.

Remove the trifle from the fridge and spoon the whipped coconut cream over the top. Return to the fridge for a couple of hours to chill, then scatter the toasted flaked almonds over the top and serve.

ALPHONSO MANGO AND LIME PAVLOVA

FOR THE MERINGUE

4 egg whites

225g caster sugar

2 teaspoons cornflour

2 teaspoons white wine vinegar

2 teaspoons vanilla extract

**FOR THE TOPPING
AND SYRUP**

50ml mango juice

Juice of 1 lime and the zest of
½ (try to get long strands
using a zester)

100g caster sugar

1 Alphonso or other ripe mango,
cut into 2-cm chunks

FOR THE CREAM

400ml coconut cream

1½ teaspoons caster sugar

Serves 6-8

Alphonso mangos are the fragrant, buttery King of India's mangos, and the Pav is the Queen of Antipodean puds. Add a thick layer of whipped coconut cream and a zesty mango and lime syrup and you have a dairy-free dessert fit for royalty. If you can't get an Alphonso (which has a short season from April-late May), then choose the ripest, juiciest mango you can. (See photograph on page 106.)

Chill the coconut cream in its carton or can in the fridge for at least 4-6 hours. Meanwhile, preheat the oven to 140°C/275°F/Gas Mark 1.

Cut out a large piece of baking parchment and draw a circle around a dinner plate on one side. Turn this upside down and place on a baking tray, greased at the corners so the parchment sticks to the tray.

Whisk the egg whites with an electric whisk in a large and scrupulously clean metal bowl (use the whisk attachment on your stand mixer, if you have one). Once stiff peaks start to form, add the sugar a spoonful at a time, continuing to whisk until all the sugar is added and incorporated. Add the cornflour, vinegar and vanilla and whisk to incorporate. The meringue mixture is ready when it is smooth, glossy and thick.

Spoon this mixture into the circle on your baking parchment, smoothing with the back of your spoon and adding extra meringue around the edges so it is shallow in the middle and taller around the edge. Make decorative peaks around the edge if you like. Bake for 1 hour, then turn off the oven and leave the meringue in to cool completely, for at least 6 hours or overnight.

Make the syrup by heating the mango juice and lime juice in saucepan over a low-medium heat. Add the sugar and bring to the boil. Boil for 3 minutes or until all the sugar has dissolved, remove from the heat and leave to cool.

Take the coconut cream out of the fridge and pour away any watery liquid. Whisk with the sugar, using an electric whisk, until thick and fluffy but not too stiff.

Once the meringue has cooled completely, carefully transfer it to a serving plate. Spoon the whipped coconut cream into the shallow centre of the meringue to form a thick layer. Arrange the mango on top, drizzle over a little of the cooled mango and lime syrup and sprinkle a little lime zest over the top. Serve with the rest of the lime and mango syrup in a jug.

AVOCADO CHOCOLATE MOUSSE

3 ripe avocados, peeled and
    stone removed
225g dark chocolate
250ml coconut cream
1 tablespoon vanilla extract
2 ½ tablespoons maple syrup

Serves 6

Avocado chocolate mousse is something of a craze on vegan blogs. This is my version, which combines a rich dark chocolate and coconut cream ganache with the creamy avocado. I know avocado chocolate mousse sounds weird and vaguely 70s, but it's one of those things you've got to try.

Mash the avocado flesh in a large bowl. Use an electric whisk or the whisk attachment of a stand mixer to whisk the flesh until it is smooth with no lumps.

Chop the dark chocolate into very small pieces and place in a large heatproof bowl.

Heat the coconut cream in a small saucepan over a medium-high heat. Remove from the heat just before it starts to boil – when you start to see bubbles form around the edges.

Pour the cream over the chocolate and stir gently with a wooden spoon until all the chocolate has melted and you have a smooth ganache. (If there is still a little chocolate which hasn't melted, then fill the empty saucepan with water and bring to a simmer – set the heatproof bowl above the saucepan so it isn't touching the water and melt the last of the chocolate, stirring gently.)

Add the vanilla extract and maple syrup and stir again until combined. Pour this mixture into the bowl with the avocado and whisk for 3-4 minutes until the mixture has a fluffy, mousse-like consistency. Divide between 6 ramekins and chill for a couple of hours before serving.

RHUBARB AND STEM GINGER CRUMBLE WITH HAZELNUTS

FOR THE FILLING

600g rhubarb, chopped into
  3-cm pieces
1 ½ tablespoons diced stem
  ginger in syrup
½ teaspoon ground cinnamon
1 ½ tablespoons golden caster
  sugar
2 tablespoons water
1 tablespoon lemon juice

FOR THE TOPPING

100g block baking margarine,
  such as Stork (NOT the
  spreadable kind), plus a little
  extra for greasing
150g plain flour
80g golden caster sugar
50g ground hazelnuts
Pinch of sea salt

Serves 4-6

At certain times of year the Call to Crumble (CTC) becomes a loud, nagging voice in my ear. The first is in autumn – when all those crisp apples and pears come into season. And the second is early spring, when bundles of fuchsia-pink rhubarb fill the shops. Try classic rhubarb crumble with a little stem ginger – it gives it a delicious kick.

Preheat the oven to 180°C/350°F/Gas Mark 4. Grease a deep circular baking dish with a little baking margarine, remove the 100g for the topping from the fridge, cut into small cubes and set aside for about 10 minutes.

Toss the rhubarb with the stem ginger, cinnamon and sugar. Arrange in the bottom of the baking dish and sprinkle the water and lemon juice on top.

Place the flour, sugar, ground hazelnuts and salt for the topping in a large bowl. Rub in the diced baking margarine gently with your fingertips just until the mixture resembles unevenly-sized breadcrumbs. Spoon the crumble topping over the fruit so it is completely covered.

Bake for 40-45 minutes, or until the fruit is tender and the topping is golden. Serve with custard or a dollop of whipped coconut cream with vanilla (both on page 137).

APPLE PIE

1 quantity sweetcrust pastry
dough (see page 142)

FOR THE FILLING
Around 525g Bramley apples
(about 2 apples), peeled,
cored and cut into 3-cm
cubes
2 red eating apples, peeled,
cored and cut into 3-cm cubes
100g golden caster sugar
1 teaspoon ground cinnamon
1 tablespoon lemon juice
1 tablespoon plain flour
1 egg, beaten
1 tablespoon dairy-free sunflower
spread

23-cm round pie dish

Serves 8

Serve up this golden-topped apple pie to the whole family – no one
will guess it's dairy-free. Just like mum used to make, but with a
sneaky bit of dairy-free spread to help make a delicious, gooey apple
sauce inside...

Make the pastry dough following the instructions on page 142 and
refrigerate for 30 minutes.

Meanwhile, for the filling, toss the apples with the sugar, cinnamon,
lemon juice and flour in a large mixing bowl and place to one side.

Place a flat baking tray on a middle shelf in the oven and preheat the
oven to 190°C/375°F/Gas Mark 5.

Lightly flour your work surface, then unwrap the larger ball of chilled
dough and roll out into a 3-mm thick circle. Line the pie dish with the
pastry, leaving a slight overhang. Brush the inside with a little beaten
egg, then fill with the apple mixture. Dot the dairy-free spread on top
of the apples.

Take the smaller ball of chilled dough and roll out in a circle on the
floured surface until it is 3-mm thick. Use your rolling pin to pick up
this circle and lay it over the top of the pie. Press the edges together
with your fingers to crimp and seal. Trim any overhang to leave a neat
edge. Brush the top of the pie with the rest of the beaten egg, then
cut a few steam holes in the top with a paring knife. Bake on top of
the heated baking tray in the centre of the oven for 40 minutes, or
until the top is golden.

Sprinkle with a little sugar, then leave to rest for 30 minutes before
serving. Serve with custard (see page 137), or ice cream (see page
120), as desired.

PUMPKIN PIE

FOR THE PASTRY
220g plain flour, plus extra for
    dusting
55g vegetable shortening,
    removed from the fridge 10
    minutes before using, diced
55g block baking margarine,
    such as Stork (NOT the
    spreadable kind), diced
1 tablespoon sugar
Good pinch of sea salt
1 medium egg yolk
Iced water

FOR THE FILLING
1 x 425-g can pumpkin purée
125g golden caster sugar
½ teaspoon ground cinnamon
½ teaspoon ground nutmeg
½ teaspoon ground ginger
2 medium eggs
200ml oat cream

23-cm round pie dish
Baking beans

Serves 8

Even the most seasoned pie-eater won't be able to tell that this pumpkin pie, with its flaky crust and creamy filling scented with cinnamon and nutmeg, is made with oat cream. Serve it at your Thanksgiving table and all the dairy-avoiders will be doubly thankful.

Sift the flour into a bowl, lifting the sieve high above the bowl to get more air into your mixture, then add the diced vegetable shortening and baking margarine. Start by using two dinner knives to work the fats into the flour until the mixture is the texture of coarse breadcrumbs, then take over with your hands, working quickly and lightly with your fingertips. Work in the sugar, salt and egg yolk.

Add enough iced water, 1 teaspoon at a time, stirring with the knife to work it in, until the mixture is just moist enough to bring together into a dough with your hands. Gather it into a ball, wrap in clingfilm and chill in the fridge for 30 minutes. Meanwhile, preheat the oven to 220°C/425°F/Gas Mark 7.

Roll out the chilled dough on a lightly floured surface into a 3-mm-thick circle. Line the pie dish with the pastry, crimping the edges with your fingertips and leaving a slight overhang. Trim any excess pastry and prick the bottom lightly all over with a fork.

Cut out a circle of baking parchment to fit inside the pie. Weigh it down with baking beans then blind bake for 10 minutes. Remove the baking beans and parchment and bake the pie crust for another 5 minutes. Remove from the oven.

Whisk together the pumpkin purée, sugar and spices in a large bowl. Whisk the eggs and oat cream together in a jug, then pour onto the pumpkin mixture and whisk until smooth. Spoon this mixture into the pie crust.

Bake in the oven for 10 minutes, then reduce the oven temperature to 180°C/350°F/Gas Mark 4 and bake for another 30 minutes, until the crust is golden and the filling is just set.

Leave to cool completely in the tin. Serve with whipped coconut cream with vanilla (see page 137).

BREAD AND 'BUTTER' PUDDING

60g currants
60g coconut oil, plus extra for
greasing
6 slices day-old white bread
50g golden caster sugar
2 large eggs
470ml almond milk
½ teaspoon ground nutmeg
1 vanilla pod (or ½ teaspoon
vanilla powder)

Approx. 26 x 18cm baking dish

Serves 4

Bread and butter pudding is a traditional British pud, often made by clever home cooks as a way to use up slightly stale bread. I've adapted my mum's recipe to make a dairy-free b&b (the butter had to go, obviously) with rich, thick coconut oil and a nutmeg-flecked almond milk batter. The result is every bit as carby and comforting (think golden, crisp bread on top and a thick, curranty custard underneath) as the original.

Soak the currants in boiling water for 10 minutes to soften and plump them up a bit. Drain and put to one side.

Warm the coconut oil in a small saucepan over a very low heat, just until it is a spreadable consistency. Spread onto each slice of bread and then cut each slice into 4 triangles. Use a little extra oil to grease a medium-sized baking dish, about 26 x 18cm.

Arrange half of the bread triangles in the bottom of the baking dish. Scatter the currants and sprinkle a third of the sugar over the slices. Top this layer with the remaining bread triangles, this time arranged in overlapping rows. Sprinkle with half the remaining sugar.

Beat the eggs and almond milk together and stir in the nutmeg. Split the vanilla pod in half with a sharp knife. Scrape out the seeds and add these to the beaten eggs and almond milk (or add the vanilla powder). Pour this mixture over the bread, leaving the tops of the top layer of bread triangles exposed. Sprinkle the remaining sugar over the top of the bread and leave to stand for 30 minutes. Meanwhile, preheat the oven to 170°C/325°F/Gas Mark

Bake or 45 minutes or until the custard is set and the bread is golden brown.

POMEGRANATE AND PROSECCO
TEACUP JELLIES

4 sheets of leaf gelatine
250ml pomegranate juice
2 tablespoons caster sugar
150ml Prosecco, Champagne or
    other sparkling wine
Handful of very fresh
    pomegranate seeds

TO SERVE (OPTIONAL)
4 teaspoons coconut yogurt
Good handful of roughly chopped
    pistachios

Makes 4

Who says dairy-eaters get all the best desserts? These jellies are a grown-up reworking of a childhood classic, with delicate and floral pomegranate juice and a hit of Prosecco, which fizzes gently on your tongue.

Soak the gelatine leaves in a bowl of cold water for 5 minutes, until soft.

Heat the pomegranate juice and sugar in a small saucepan over a medium heat. Remove the softened gelatine leaves from the bowl, wring out any excess water and add to the juice and sugar. Stir until dissolved, then remove from the heat. Pour in the Prosecco, stir once just to combine, then set aside to cool.

When the liquid is cool enough to go into the fridge, decant into a jug and pour into pretty tea cups or small glasses. Chill for 1-1 ½ hours, until thickened but not completely set, then remove from the fridge and add a scattering of pomegranate seeds to each. You may need to stir them in a little. Chill for at least another 3 hours, or overnight.

Serve with a dollop of coconut yogurt and a smattering of chopped pistachios, if you like.

COCONUT MILK ICE CREAM

5 egg yolks
75g golden caster sugar
2 teaspoons cornflour
300ml coconut milk
200ml coconut cream

FOR VANILLA FLAVOUR
Seeds of 1 vanilla pod or
 ½-1 teaspoon vanilla powder
 (optional)
½ teaspoon vanilla extract

**FOR CINNAMON CRUNCH
FLAVOUR**
1 tablespoon vanilla extract
½ teaspoon ground cinnamon
35g crunchy cinnamon cereal
 flakes (such as Curiously
 Cinnamon), roughly chopped
 into small pieces (check the
 label to make sure it's
 dairy-free)

Ice-cream maker

Makes about 600ml

This ice cream is so luscious and creamy that you'll never hanker after the store-bought stuff again. Once you've mastered the coconut base, you can leave the vanilla out if you want to play up the coconut flavour – to make a coconut and mango ice cream for example. Or you can make the cinnamon crunch variation. It's the contrast between the smooth, creamy base and the buried treasure of the golden nuggets that makes this cinnamon ice cream ridiculously addictive.

Whisk the egg yolks, sugar and cornflour together in a bowl.

Pour the coconut milk and cream into a saucepan and stir in the vanilla seeds or powder, if using, and the vanilla extract. Heat until simmering over a low-medium heat, removing it just when it starts to bubble around the edges of the pan; don't let it boil.

Pour onto the egg yolk and sugar mixture in a slow, steady stream, whisking constantly with a balloon whisk to combine. Once you've got a smooth custard, return it to the pan and cook over a very low heat, stirring with a wooden spoon, until it is moderately thick – be patient and don't be tempted to turn the heat up, it will thicken eventually. It's thick enough when it can pass the spoon test: when the custard coats the back of your wooden spoon and you run a finger down the back of it, it should leave a clear line. Remove from the heat and leave to cool.

Once cooled, churn in an ice-cream maker according to the instructions. Pour into an airtight container and freeze for a couple of hours before serving. Any extra ice cream will store in the freezer for up to 2 weeks.

FOR CINNAMON CRUNCH FLAVOUR
Prepare the ice cream as above, adding the vanilla and ground cinnamon with the coconut milk and cream in the saucepan. Continue as instructed until the ice cream has churned in the ice-cream maker. At this stage, when it is a soft-serve consistency, fold in the cinnamon cereal pieces. Freeze as above.

ESPRESSO AND RAW CHOCOLATE GRANITA

400ml freshly-brewed,
 good-quality espresso,
 piping hot
75g caster sugar
30g cacao nibs

Serves 6

Granita is gelato's ristretto-drinking, all-black-wearing sibling. The dessert – sweet ice crystals typically flavoured with lemon, coffee or orange – is originally from Sicily but there are variations all over Italy. Serve in delicate glasses.

Pour the espresso over the sugar in a large bowl and stir until all the sugar has dissolved. Leave to cool.

Once cool, pour the mixture into a freezerproof plastic tub or ceramic baking dish – you're looking for something wide and fairly shallow.

Freeze flat on a shelf of your freezer for 2 hours. Use a fork to rake through the mixture – right now it has a Slush Puppie texture but you want to break it up so it forms ice crystals. Return to freezer and repeat this process every half hour – another 3 or 4 times – until the entire mixture has formed into ice crystals.

Remove the mixture from the freezer and use your fork to stir in most of the cacao nibs. Hold some back to sprinkle on top of each serving.

Divide the mixture between small glasses or ramekins and serve immediately.

PANNA COTTA

3 sheets of leaf gelatine
400ml almond milk
75g golden caster sugar
Seeds from ½ vanilla pod or
    ¼ teaspoon vanilla powder
½ teaspoon vanilla extract

Serves 4

Here's that classic dessert, reinvented without the dairy. Because almond milk is blended with water, these panna cottas are a little delicate. Give them a good 4-6 hours to set in the fridge and, if you're nervous about turning them out onto plates, serve them in their ramekins.

Soak the gelatine leaves in a bowl of cold water for 5 minutes, or until soft.

Put the almond milk in a saucepan over a medium heat. Whisk in the sugar and vanilla seeds or powder and the vanilla extract. Bring to a simmer, check that all the sugar has dissolved, then remove from the heat.

Remove the softened gelatine leaves from the bowl of water, wring out any excess water and add to the almond milk mixture, stirring until completely dissolved.

Divide the mixture between 4 small ramekins, greased with just a dab of vegetable oil. Alternatively you can use espresso cups with round bottoms or dariole moulds if you have them. Leave to cool, then chill in the fridge for 4-6 hours, or until set but still with a good jiggle.

Remove from the fridge. Pour hot water into a shallow baking dish and carefully dunk each ramekin, mould or cup into the water for a few seconds, then turn out onto a small plate. They should come out easily, but if not then dunk the ramekin in the hot water again or run a very sharp knife (that has been dipped in boiling water) around the inside edge of the ramekin to loosen the panna cotta. Alternatively, serve in the dishes.

Serve with fresh berries or compote.

ROSE AND CARDAMOM RICE PUDDING

Couple of handfuls of unsalted
    pistachios
1 tablespoon coconut oil
120g pudding rice
400ml coconut milk
200ml water
50g golden caster sugar
4 cardamom pods, lightly
    crushed with the back
    of a knife
½ teaspoon rosewater
Edible rose petals (optional)

*Serves 4 (restaurant-size
portions as this pudding is
rather rich)*

A simple, stovetop rice pudding made with coconut milk, studded with
pistachios and gorgeously fragrant with rose and cardamom. Dairy-
free nerd fact: rice pudding is synonymous with dairy now, but did you
know that in medieval times it was made with almond milk?

Toast the pistachios in a small, dry frying pan over a medium heat
until golden. Keep a careful eye on them as they can burn quickly.
Remove from the heat, transfer to a chopping board to cool, then
roughly chop.

Heat the coconut oil in a large, heavy-bottomed saucepan over a
low-medium heat. Once melted, add the rice and stir to coat. Cook
for 1 minute, pour in the coconut milk and water, then stir in the sugar
and cardamom pods.

Bring to the boil, then turn the heat down and simmer for 20 minutes,
stirring regularly, until the rice grains are tender and plumped up and
the liquid has reduced by around half. Pour in a little more water if
needed. Remove the cardamom pods, stir in the rosewater and fold in
half of the chopped pistachios.

Leave to cool for 10 minutes, then serve while still warm, decorated
with the remaining chopped pistachios and a few edible rose petals,
if using. Or leave to cool completely, chill in the fridge and serve
completely cold.

BANANAS FOSTER

3 tablespoons coconut oil
½ teaspoon ground cinnamon
60g soft brown sugar
4 tablespoons dark rum
4 medium bananas, peeled and
   cut lengthways into quarters
4 scoops of coconut milk ice
   cream (see page 120)

Serves 4

This kitsch confection of bananas, booze and ice cream hails from New Orleans. Traditionally the bananas are caramelised with butter, but coconut oil is an ideal alternative - its flavour pairs perfectly with the sticky bananas and rum sauce. It's just begging to be served with a paper umbrella and a couple of hanging cocktail monkeys.

Melt the coconut oil in a large, heavy-bottomed frying pan over a medium heat and, as soon as it's melted, stir in the cinnamon and sugar and cook until all the clumps have gone from the sugar and you have a smooth, thick paste.

Add 1 tablespoon of the rum and stir to combine. Spread the banana quarters out in the pan and fry until sticky and turning golden, turning them over with kitchen tongs halfway through to make sure they are golden all over.

Remove the pan from the heat and gently pour in the remaining rum. Tilt the pan away from you and carefully use a long match or candle lighter to flambé the bananas until the flames die out.

Divide the ice cream between four sundae bowls. Add the banana pieces to each bowl using kitchen tongs, then pour over the rum sauce.

LEMON 'CHEESE'CAKE

FOR THE GRAHAM CRACKER BASE

1 x quantity Graham crackers (see page 132, but replace the cinnamon with 2 teaspoons ground ginger, and use a plain round or square cookie cutter)

120g dairy-free sunflower spread, melted and cooled

FOR THE TOPPING

550g vegan cream cheese, such as Tofutti, chilled

250ml coconut cream, chilled for at least 4 hours

125g icing sugar, sifted

Finely grated zest and juice of 2 ½ lemons, plus extra zest, finely pared, to serve

20-cm round, springform cake tin

Serves 8-10

It's cheesecake, Jim, but not as you know it. Take a homemade Graham cracker base (very similar to British digestives in taste and texture) with ground ginger, and top with a velvety layer of vegan cream cheese, whipped into a mousse-like texture with coconut cream and lots of lemon. Delicious.

Roughly break up 300g of the Graham crackers, then whizz into fine crumbs in a food processor (or put into a large, sealed freezer bag and have a good bash with the end of a rolling pin until you have fine crumbs).

Transfer the crumbs to a large bowl and stir in the melted sunflower spread. Tip the mixture into the bottom of the cake tin and press down firmly with a wooden spoon so you have a compact crust with a smooth top. Chill for 30 minutes.

Meanwhile, to make the topping, whisk together the vegan cream cheese, chilled coconut cream (drain away any liquid from the can or carton first), icing sugar and lemon juice for 3-4 minutes, using an electric mixer or the paddle attachment of a stand mixer, until fluffy and any clumps of icing sugar have gone. Fold in the lemon zest with a large metal spoon.

Take the cheesecake base out of the fridge and spoon the topping over the top. Smooth the surface with a spatula or palette knife and return to the fridge to chill for at least 4 hours before serving. To serve, just remove the sides from the tin and sprinkle lemon zest over the top.

SALTY CARAMEL POPCORN

1 ½ tablespoons sunflower or
    vegetable oil
100g popping corn
Pinch of sea salt

FOR THE CARAMEL
40g soft brown sugar
4 tablespoons golden syrup
2 tablespoons coconut oil
1 teaspoon water
Sea salt

Serves 2 greedy people

It's the age-old dilemma: salty or sweet popcorn? This rich, salted caramel corn is for all those who can't decide. Just add a black-and-white movie, a quilt and someone to cosy up to for the perfect movie night...

Heat the oil in a large, heavy-based saucepan over a medium heat. Pour in the corn and flake in the sea salt. Put the lid on the pan. The corn will start popping after about 1 minute and carry on for another 2-3 minutes.

When the popping sounds slow down to longer than 4 or 5 seconds between pops, remove from the heat and leave to cool slightly in the pan.

Meanwhile, for the caramel, put the sugar, syrup, coconut oil and water in a saucepan over a medium-high heat. Stir constantly with a wooden spoon until the coconut oil has melted and the sugar dissolved. Bring to the boil and let it bubble rapidly for 4-5 minutes, stirring constantly, until the mixture is a dark, reddish toffee colour.

Tip the popcorn into a large heatproof bowl. Pour the toffee sauce over the popcorn and stir well to coat all the kernels. Leave to cool slightly and let the toffee sauce harden for around 5-10 minutes, then sprinkle with sea salt, stir again and dig in.

CHOCOLATE TRUFFLES

200g dark chocolate
175ml coconut cream
1 tablespoon rum
Cocoa powder, finely chopped
   nuts or desiccated coconut,
   to coat

Makes around 20

Sometimes it's the little things that can bother you about living dairy-free. Like having to forgo those dainty truffles which come with coffee in smart restaurants, or having to turn down chocolate in the office. So why not make your own truffles? They're really easy - as long as you can cope with a bit of melted chocolate on your kitchen surfaces - and make thoughtful gifts, too. I've made these with rum, but you could try espresso, mint essence, bourbon, orange - have fun experimenting.

Chop the chocolate into very small pieces and place in a large heatproof bowl.

Heat the coconut cream in a small saucepan over a medium-high heat. Remove from the heat just as it comes to the boil - as soon as it starts bubbling around the edges.

Pour the cream over the chocolate and stir gently with a wooden spoon until all the chocolate has melted and you have a smooth, thick ganache. (If there is still a little chocolate that hasn't melted, then fill the empty saucepan with water and bring to a simmer - set the bowl above the saucepan so it isn't touching the water and melt the last of the chocolate, stirring gently.)

Stir in the rum and chill in the fridge for 4 hours.

Place your chosen coating/s in a dessert bowl/s and line a baking tray with greaseproof paper.

Remove the truffle mixture from the fridge. If you have one, dip a melon baller in very hot water, then use it to scoop out truffle-sized balls from the chocolate mixture. Pour a little more hot water over the melon baller between each go. Or use a teaspoon and roll the chocolate between your palms to form a ball (be warned, this gets pretty messy). Roll each truffle in the coating of your choice, then place on the baking tray. Return to the fridge and chill until ready to serve, or to package as gifts.

S'MORES WITH HOMEMADE GRAHAM CRACKERS

FOR THE GRAHAM CRACKERS
175g wholegrain spelt flour
175g plain flour, plus extra for
    dusting
1 teaspoon ground cinnamon
1 teaspoon baking powder
Pinch of sea salt
200g block baking margarine,
    such as Stork (NOT the
    spreadable kind), at room
    temperature
170g soft brown sugar
1 tablespoon honey
1 egg

FOR THE S'MORES
Dark chocolate
Marshmallows

2 baking trays lined with
    greaseproof paper

*Makes about 20 biscuits/
10 S'mores*

Campfire bananas filled with cheap chocolate were the culinary highlight of my Brownies days. Meanwhile in America, they had it made – Graham crackers crammed with chocolate and a marshmallow all toasty and melty from the campfire. Just add a campfire (or grill) and your best ghost stories...

Sift the flours, cinnamon, baking powder and salt together.

Cream the vegetable margarine, sugar and honey together with a wooden spoon until pale and fluffy. Whisk in the egg and 1 tablespoon of the flour. Fold in the rest of the flour mixture with a large wooden spoon until combined. Bring the biscuit dough together into a ball, wrap in clingfilm and chill for 30 minutes. Meanwhile, preheat the oven to 180°C/350°F/Gas Mark 4.

Lightly dust the work surface and rolling pin with flour. Roll out the chilled dough into a rectangle about 3mm thick.

Use a 6-cm square, fluted cookie cutter to cut the Graham crackers out. For extra authenticity, use a toothpick or the tines of a fork to make a few rows of evenly-spaced holes in the middle of each. Space each cracker well apart on the baking trays and bake for 12-15 minutes, turning the trays round halfway through cooking time, until nut-brown. Remove from the oven and leave to cool completely.

To make the S'mores over a campfire, top half of the crackers with a piece of chocolate about the same size as the cracker. Toast the marshmallows on long sticks until golden and gooey. Place a marshmallow on top of the chocolate, place another Graham cracker on top and press down for a minute to melt the chocolate slightly.

To make indoors, place half the crackers on a lined baking tray. Top each with a piece of chocolate about the same size as the cracker. Heat the grill and line another baking tray with foil. Space out the marshmallows (you need one for each S'more) and grill for about 10 seconds until golden on one top, then carefully turn onto their sides using kitchen tongs and grill. Remove from the heat and place a marshmallow on top of the chocolate, place another Graham cracker on top and press down for 10 seconds, then leave for a minute to melt the chocolate slightly. Eat immediately.

DISHOOM'S BOMBAY COLADA

FOR THE SYRUP *Serves 8-10*

1 cinnamon stick
1 whole nutmeg
2 cloves
2 cardamom pods
1 vanilla pod
250g sugar
2.5-cm piece of ginger, peeled
    and grated
125ml water

FOR THE COLADA *Serves 1*

20ml chai syrup (see above)
90ml coconut cream
70ml pineapple juice
20ml fresh lime juice
10 coriander leaves
200g ice cubes
25ml good-quality rum (optional)
Dash of Violette liqueur
    (optional)

TO GARNISH (OPTIONAL)

Pineapple leaf
Candy fennel seeds

Serves 1

Dishoom is an excellent Indian restaurant in London, where the cocktails are as delicious as the daal. I have a mild addiction to its Bombay Colada – a spice-infused take on the guilty-pleasure Piña Colada (think notes of cardamom and ginger, rather than glacé cherries and cocktail umbrellas). This luscious concoction is the brainchild of Carl Brown at Dishoom, who normally makes the Bombay syrup in 5-litre batches. Below is a scaled-down version to make at home, with or without rum.

Make the syrup the night before. Toast the cinnamon stick, nutmeg and cloves in a small, dry, heavy-bottomed frying pan over a medium heat – just until they start to release their aromas. Keep a careful eye on the pan so they don't burn. Remove from the heat and leave to cool.

Make a crack in each cardamom pod by scoring with a knife. Split open the vanilla pod with a sharp knife but don't remove the seeds.

Put the sugar in a large bowl and add the cardamom, vanilla, ginger, cinnamon, nutmeg and cloves. Massage them all into the sugar with your fingertips.

Put the water in a large saucepan and bring to the boil. Once at boiling point, tip in the sugar mixture and keep stirring until all the sugar crystals have dissolved. Remove from the heat and pour into a large jug or bowl. Cover and leave to cool and infuse overnight.

The next day, pour the syrup through a fine-mesh sieve into a jug, to strain and remove the spices.

To make a Virgin Colada, put 20ml of this syrup, plus the coconut cream, pineapple juice, lime juice, coriander and ice in a blender, and whizz until thick and smooth. Pour into a hi-ball glass.

To make an alcoholic version, add the rum to the bottom of the hi-ball glass first, then pour the Colada mixture on top, whisking briefly combine. Discard any extra Colada mixture so you have enough room to splash the Violette over the top, if using. Garnish, if you like, with a pineapple leaf and candy fennel seeds. (Store any leftover syrup in an airtight container in the fridge for up to 2 weeks.)

ULTIMATE HOT CHOCOLATE

250ml hazelnut milk
60g dark chocolate, chopped into
  small pieces
1½ teaspoons cocoa powder
½ teaspoon maple syrup
¼ teaspoon vanilla extract or
  pinch of cinnamon (both
  optional)
Pinch of salt

*Makes 2 cups, or 4-6 espresso
shots*

A rich, giddy-making cup of chocolate, closer in spirit to Montezuma II's goblets of *xocolatl*, than those watery brews made with instant chocolate powder. Only the hardiest chocaholic will be able to handle more than a cup...

Warm 100ml of the hazelnut milk in a heavy-bottomed saucepan over a low-medium heat. Add the dark chocolate pieces and stir with a wooden spoon until they have melted. Slowly pour in the rest of the hazelnut milk, stirring to combine, then whisk in the cocoa powder. Turn the heat up to medium, add the maple syrup, vanilla or cinnamon, if using, and the salt and bring almost – but not to – boiling point.

Pour into cups or espresso cups and drink immediately.

CHOCOLATE SAUCE

100g dark chocolate
4 tablespoons coconut cream
1 tablespoon dairy-free sunflower
  spread
½ tablespoon maple syrup
½ teaspoon vanilla extract
Pinch of sea salt

Serves 4

Every cook needs a classic chocolate sauce recipe up their sleeve and this is the dairy-free version (not that your guests need know that, unless you want them to)...

Bring a pan half-filled with water to a gentle simmer over a low-medium heat. Put the chocolate and coconut cream in a heatproof bowl that will sit above – but not touching – the water. Stir until melted, then stir in the dairy-free spread, maple syrup and vanilla until you have a thick and glossy sauce. If it looks in any danger of splitting, take off the heat and stir.

Stir in the salt then remove from the heat and allow to cool for 5 minutes before serving warm.

SALTED CARAMEL SAUCE

4 tablespoons coconut oil
80g soft brown sugar
½ teaspoon vanilla extract
1½ tablespoons coconut cream
Pinch of sea salt

Serves 4 (makes around 200ml)

Salted caramel: two words to make this grown-woman go weak at the knees. There's something about the juxtaposition of achingly-sweet caramel with a little sea salt that always proves irresistible. Drizzle it over coconut milk ice cream (see page 120) or dark chocolate cake...

Heat the coconut oil and sugar in a saucepan over a medium-high heat, stirring constantly with a wooden spoon until the coconut oil has melted and the sugar dissolved. Stir in the vanilla extract and coconut cream, sprinkle in the sea salt and simmer for a couple of minutes until you have a smooth and creamy sauce.

CUSTARD

4 egg yolks
1 ½ tablespoons golden caster
    sugar
2 teaspoons cornflour
400ml soya or coconut milk
Seeds from 1 vanilla pod or
    ½ teaspoon vanilla powder

Serves 4-6

A creamy, luscious custard flecked with vanilla seeds.

Whisk the egg yolks, sugar and cornflour together in a bowl.

Pour the soya or coconut milk into a saucepan and stir in the vanilla. Heat until simmering over a low-medium heat, removing it just when it starts to bubble around the edges of the pan; don't let it boil.

Pour onto the egg yolk and sugar mixture in a slow, steady stream, whisking constantly with a balloon whisk to combine. Once you've got a smooth custard, return it to the pan and cook over a very low heat, stirring with a wooden spoon, until it thickens to your desired consistency.

Pour into a jug and serve immediately.

WHIPPED COCONUT CREAM

250ml coconut cream
1 tablespoon caster sugar
1 teaspoon vanilla extract
    (optional)

Makes 250ml, or serves
4-6 alongside dessert

Whipped coconut cream is an incredibly useful dairy-free topping – and it's delicious. The trick is to leave a carton of coconut cream in the fridge as long as possible to thicken up, and to drain away any coconut water before you start to whip it. It doesn't whip up quite as stiff as double cream would but it's thick enough to use on desserts, with waffles, and on top of scones and trifles. Use vanilla extract when you want to pair it with traditional desserts, like sponge cakes, and leave it out when you want the coconut flavour to come through, as in the mango and lime pavlova on page 112.

Chill the coconut cream in its carton or can in the fridge for at least 4-6 hours and preferably overnight.

Take the coconut cream out of the fridge and pour away any watery liquid. Whisk the coconut cream and sugar together, and the vanilla extract if using, with an electric mixer, until thick and fluffy. Use immediately.

BAKING

BROWNIES

225g dark chocolate,
   70% cocoa solids
260g light muscovado sugar
200ml sunflower oil
50g cocoa powder
½ teaspoon gluten-free baking
   powder
Pinch of sea salt
50g ground hazelnuts
3 eggs, lightly beaten

20-cm square tin, greased
   and lined

Makes 16 squares

"What devilment is this? Witchcraft!" joked my husband when I first told him these brownies were not just dairy- but gluten-free, too. These squidgy, fudgy brownies with a proper crust are made with ground hazelnuts and plenty of 70% dark chocolate. No witchcraft, just good ingredients.

Preheat the oven to 180°C/350°F/Gas Mark 4.

Chop 200g of the chocolate into small chunks. Half-fill a saucepan with water and heat over a low-medium heat until simmering. Put the chocolate chunks, sugar and 100ml of the oil in a heatproof bowl and place it so it is resting on the rim of the saucepan, but not touching the water. Stir with a wooden spoon until all the chocolate has melted. Remove from the heat and set aside to cool a little.

Meanwhile, chop the remaining 25g of chocolate into chocolate-chip-sized chunks and place to one side. Sift the cocoa powder, baking powder and salt together in a separate bowl and stir in the ground hazelnuts.

Using an electric whisk, or the paddle attachment of a stand mixer, gradually add the beaten eggs, 2 tablespoons of the cocoa powder mixture and the remaining oil to the melted chocolate mixture until they are all combined and you have a glossy mixture.

Fold in the remaining cocoa powder mixture with a large metal spoon just until combined. Stir in the chocolate chip pieces.

Spoon the mixture into the prepared tin, smooth the surface and bake for 25–30 minutes until the top has formed a crust and the inside is cooked but still fudgy. Allow to cool for at least an hour in the tin before cutting into squares.

SHORTCRUST PASTRY

FOR SWEETCRUST PASTRY

300g plain flour
75g vegetable shortening,
   removed from the fridge 10
   minutes before using, diced
75g block baking margarine, such
   as Stork (NOT the spreadable
   kind), chilled and diced
2 tablespoons caster sugar
1 egg yolk
Pinch of salt
Iced water

*Makes 500g, enough to line and
top a 23-cm pie*

Make everything from blueberry pies to pasties with this versatile shortcrust pastry. There are 2 variations – a sweetcrust to use in dishes like the apple pie on page 115, and a savoury shortcrust which you can make with lard for great flavour, or baking margarine if you're vegetarian. Vegetable shortening is very hard when removed from the fridge, so taking it out 10 minutes before you start making the pastry ensures it's still cold but just softened enough to work with.

Sift the flour into a mixing bowl (lift the sieve high above the bowl to get more air into your mixture), then add the diced vegetable shortening and baking margarine. Start by using 2 dinner knives to work the shortening into the flour until it is the texture of coarse breadcrumbs, then take over with your hands, working quickly and lightly with your fingertips. Work in the sugar, egg yolk and salt.

Add the iced water, a teaspoon at a time, and stir with the knife to work into the mixture. Only continue to add it until the mixture is just moist enough to bring together with your hands to form a dough. Gather it into a ball, wrap in clingfilm and refrigerate for 30 minutes before using.

FOR SAVOURY PASTRY

300g plain flour
Pinch of salt
75g vegetable shortening,
   removed from the fridge 10
   minutes before using, diced
75g lard, chilled and diced
   (or you can use block baking
   margarine to make the pastry
   vegetarian or vegan)
Iced water

*Makes 500g, enough to line and
top a 23-cm pie*

Make as above, but omit the egg yolk and sugar, and add the salt with the flour.

LEMON CURD

4 eggs, plus 2 egg yolks
2 teaspoons cornflour
100g dairy-free sunflower spread
Grated zest of 2 lemons, plus the
    juice of 3
175g golden caster sugar
Pinch of sea salt

Makes 1 jar

A truly voluptuous lemon curd to spread on toast, in a Victoria sandwich or in the show-stopping lemon meringue sponge on page 156...

Beat the whole eggs, yolks and cornflour together in a large bowl and place to one side.

Put the dairy-free spread in a saucepan over a medium heat, stirring until it starts to melt.

Add the lemon zest, juice, sugar and salt. Keep stirring constantly until the spread has all melted and the sugar has dissolved. Strain through a sieve into another pan or large bowl and return the strained liquid to the pan over a low-medium heat.

Pour in the beaten egg mixture in a slow, steady stream, whisking constantly to combine. Keep whisking until the mixture has the consistency of thick custard.

Remove from the heat. Leave to cool completely then pour into a sterilised jar and seal. Store in the fridge and use within 1 week.

A PROPER AFTERNOON TEA

1. SCONES

225g self-raising flour, plus extra
    for dusting
1 teaspoon baking powder
½ teaspoon sea salt
60g block baking margarine such
    as Stork (NOT the spreadable
    kind), removed from the fridge
    15 minutes before using, diced
25g golden caster sugar
120ml almond or soya milk,
    plus extra for brushing

TO SERVE
Jam
1 quantity whipped coconut
    cream with vanilla
    (see page 137)

Makes 6 large scones

No afternoon tea would be complete without freshly baked scones, still warm from the oven. Slather them with jam and top with a dollop of coconut whipped cream. A big pot of tea is, of course, mandatory.

Preheat the oven to 220°C/425°F/Gas Mark 7 and grease a baking tray.

Sift the flour, baking powder and salt into a bowl. Lightly rub the baking margarine into the flour with your fingertips (make sure you have cold hands for this bit), just until the mixture resembles large breadcrumbs. Mix in the sugar with your fingertips.

Pour in the almond or soya milk a little at a time (you may not need all of it) and bring the mixture together into a dough.

Lightly flour the work surface and roll out the dough gently with a rolling pin (don't press down too hard) to a thickness of 2cm. Cut out the scones using a round 6-cm cutter.

Brush the tops of the scones with a little almond or soya milk. Space out on the prepared baking tray and bake for 10-12 minutes until well risen and golden. Leave to cool on a wire rack.

Serve with a layer of jam topped by a dollop of the whipped coconut cream (or the other way around, if so inclined).

2. EGG AND CHIVE FINGER SANDWICHES

2 eggs
1 tablespoon good-quality
  mayonnaise (check the label to
  make sure it's dairy-free)
Small handful of chives, finely
  chopped
4 thin slices soft white bread,
  crusts removed
Sea salt and freshly ground
  black pepper

Makes 8

These dainty sandwiches are a must at any proper afternoon tea.
Arrange them in neat, Jenga-style stacks on your tea stand.

Hard-boil the eggs, then leave to cool for 10 minutes before peeling.
Roughly chop into small pieces with a fork in a mixing bowl. Stir in the
mayonnaise and then the chives. Season and then spread onto half
the slices of bread. Top with the other slices, cut into neat rectangles
and serve immediately.

3. SMOKED SALMON FINGER SANDWICHES

2 large slices smoked salmon
Lemon juice
4 thin slices soft white bread,
  crusts removed
Freshly ground black pepper

Makes 8

Keep smoked salmon sandwiches dairy-free by omitting the butter or
spread. After all, they're going to be eaten immediately and no one
wants the aftertaste of marg spoiling all that beautiful salmon.

Trim any rough edges off the smoked salmon and cut into smaller
slices if needed. Squeeze a little lemon juice on the salmon and grind
a little black pepper on top.

Place the slices of smoked salmon onto two of the slices of bread.
Place the other slices of bread on top and cut into neat rectangles.
Serve immediately.

4. VICTORIA SANDWICH

245ml rapeseed oil
225g golden caster sugar
4 medium eggs
225g self-raising flour, sifted
1 tablespoon vanilla extract
Icing sugar, for dusting

FOR THE FILLING
250ml coconut cream
1 teaspoon vanilla extract
1 tablespoon caster sugar
Fresh strawberries OR
   raspberry jam

2 x 20cm round cake tins,
   greased and lined

Serves 10-12

The Victoria sandwich is the cornerstone of British baking – a simple sponge, spread with cream or buttercream and sandwiched together with jam. It's just too good to live without on a dairy-free diet. Luckily, this golden sponge, sandwiched with pillowy whipped coconut cream and fresh strawberries (or jam, if you prefer), is every bit as delicious as a classic Victoria sandwich – and I've tried it out on lots of committed butter-eaters!

Chill the coconut cream for the filling in its carton or can in the fridge for at least 4-6 hours and preferably overnight.

Preheat the oven to 180ºC/350ºF/Gas Mark 4.

Beat the oil and sugar together using an electric whisk or the paddle attachment of a stand mixer for a few minutes, until well combined.

Add the eggs one at a time, alternating with a tablespoon of the flour each time and whisking to combine. Whisk in the vanilla and fold in the remaining flour, using a large metal spoon, until just combined.

Spoon the cake batter into the prepared tins. Smooth the tops, then bake on the middle shelf of the oven for 20-25 minutes, or until the tops are golden and a skewer or cocktail stick inserted into the middles comes out clean.

Leave to cool for 5 minutes in the tins, before turning out onto a wire rack to cool completely.

Meanwhile, take the coconut cream out of the fridge and pour away any watery liquid. Whisk with the vanilla and sugar, using a hand-held electric whisk or whisk attachment of a stand mixer, until thick and fluffy. Return the cream to the fridge until the cake is completely cool.

Slice the strawberries, if using, and arrange on the surface of the cake you want to go on the bottom, or spread raspberry jam over the surface. Spoon coconut cream onto the other cake, leaving a small border around the edge of the cake (you probably won't need all the cream). Sandwich the two together gently, sift a little icing sugar over the top of the cake and serve.

BLACK AND WHITE COOKIES

175g golden caster sugar
115g dairy-free sunflower spread
320g plain flour
30g cornflour
½ teaspoon baking powder
Pinch of salt
2 eggs
½ teaspoon vanilla extract
170ml almond milk
Grated zest of ½ lemon

FOR THE ICING
240g icing sugar
250g dairy-free sunflower spread
Approx. ½ teaspoon vanilla
    extract
4 ½ tablespoons cocoa powder

Makes 10 large cookies

Black and white cookies are as New York as the Empire State Building and sweary taxi drivers. They even cameo'd in a Seinfeld plot. You'll find them shrink-wrapped on the counter of every deli and bodega in the city, but those fondant-smothered versions are rarely a patch on those made in family-run bakeries. I much prefer them with frosting and stippled with lemon zest, the way they serve them at Glaser's Bake Shop, a 100-year-old bakery on the Upper East Side.

Preheat the oven to 190°C/375°F/Gas Mark 5. Grease and line 2 baking trays.

Cream together the sugar and dairy-free spread with a wooden spoon in a large bowl, until pale and fluffy.

Sift the flour, cornflour, baking powder and salt together in a separate bowl. Add one of the eggs, the vanilla extract, and 1 tablespoon of the flour mixture to the creamed sugar mixture and beat with an electric whisk, or paddle attachment of a stand mixer, until combined. Whisk in the second egg and the almond milk.

Fold the remaining flour mixture into the batter with a large metal spoon, then fold in the lemon zest.

Using an ice-cream scoop, place a scoop of cookie dough on one of the prepared baking trays and flatten down gently into a circle with the back of the scoop. Repeat with the remaining dough, so you have 5 on each tray, spacing the cookies well apart. Bake for 15–20 minutes until golden, then leave to cool on the baking trays for 5 minutes, before turning out onto a wire rack to cool completely. (These have a cakey texture, not a crumbly one.)

When the cookies are completely cool, make the icing. Cream together the icing sugar and dairy-free spread with an electric whisk or paddle attachment of a stand mixer until creamy and smooth, with no lumps (this will take a few minutes). Transfer half to a separate bowl and stir in the vanilla extract. Whisk the cocoa powder into the other half.

Place a piece of greaseproof paper with a straight edge halfway across each cookie. Use a small spatula or palette knife to smooth the chocolate icing onto one half of all the cookies. Repeat with a clean spatula, icing all the other halves with the vanilla icing.

SHORTBREAD

290g block baking margarine,
  such as Stork (NOT the
  spreadable kind), at room
  temperature, diced
120g golden caster sugar,
  plus extra for sprinkling
½ teaspoon vanilla extract
270g plain flour, sifted
110g rice flour, sifted
Good pinch of sea salt

26 x 19cm baking tin,
  greased and lined

Makes 20 slices

Make a big pot of tea and help yourself to a slice or three of this crisp and crumbly shortbread.

Beat the baking margarine, sugar and vanilla together in a large bowl, using a wooden spoon, until pale and fluffy.

Sift together the flours and salt and add to the creamed mixture. Fold together using a large metal spoon and then bring together with your hands into a smooth dough.

Place the dough in the prepared tin and press down lightly with your palm or the back of a wooden spoon to make a smooth, flat layer. Chill in the fridge for 30 minutes. Meanwhile, preheat the oven to 170°C/325°F/Gas Mark 3.

Bake for 40 minutes or until lightly golden. Remove from the oven, sprinkle with a little sugar and score about 20 slices with a sharp knife. Leave to cool completely in the tin before cutting the slices with the sharp knife. Store any leftover shortbread in an airtight tin – it will keep for a few days.

CHOCOLATE BIRTHDAY CAKE

175g self-raising flour, sifted
50g cocoa powder
1 teaspoon baking powder
Pinch of salt
245ml rapeseed or vegetable oil
225g golden caster sugar
4 medium eggs

FOR THE GANACHE
300g dark chocolate, finely
    chopped
425ml coconut cream, room
    temperature
2 tablespoons icing sugar, sifted
75ml coconut cream, chilled

TO DECORATE
Multi-coloured sprinkles/
    hundreds and thousands

2 x 20-cm round cake/sandwich
    tins, greased and lined

Serves 6-8

This is everything a good chocolate cake should be: a light and moist sponge, creamy chocolate filling and a rich, glossy ganache icing. And sprinkles - everybody loves sprinkles. (See photograph on page 138.)

Preheat the oven to 180°C/350°F/Gas Mark 4. Sift the self-raising flour, cocoa, baking powder and salt together in a large mixing bowl. Beat the oil and sugar together with an electric whisk, or with the paddle attachment of a stand mixer, for a few minutes, until well combined. Add the eggs one at a time, alternating with a tablespoon of the flour and cocoa mixture, and whisk to combine. Fold in the rest of the flour using a large metal spoon, until just combined.

Divide the cake batter between the 2 tins. Smooth the tops, then bake on the middle shelf of the preheated oven for 20-25 minutes, or until the tops are golden brown and a skewer or cocktail stick inserted into the middles comes out clean. Leave to cool for 5 minutes in the tins before turning out onto a wire rack to cool completely.

Once the cakes have cooled, make the ganache. Heat the coconut cream in a saucepan over a medium-high heat. Remove from the heat just as it comes to the boil - as soon as it starts bubbling around the edges. Put the chocolate pieces in a heatproof bowl, pour the coconut cream over and stir gently with a wooden spoon until all the chocolate has melted and you have a smooth, thick ganache. (If there is still a little chocolate that hasn't melted, then fill the empty pan with water, bring to a simmer and set the bowl above the saucepan so it isn't touching the water, to melt the last of the chocolate, stirring gently.) Whisk in the icing sugar. Transfer 8 tablespoons of ganache to a separate, smaller bowl. Refrigerate both bowls for 10 minutes.

Remove the smaller bowl of ganache from the fridge. Add the chilled 75ml coconut cream (pour away any remaining watery liquid) and whisk with an electric mixer/paddle attachment of a stand mixer until it is a pale, milk chocolate shade and mousse-y in texture, with the consistency of double cream. Spread over the centre of one of the cakes, leaving a 1cm gap around the edge of the cake. Place the other cake on the top. Remove the remaining ganache from the fridge and spread over the top of the cake, letting it spill over the sides. Use a palette knife or spatula to smooth the sides to give you your base coat of icing. Spread on a second layer to cover any patches where you can still see the sponge, and smooth again. The cake should now be completely covered with ganache, with no sponge visible. Decorate with sprinkles. Leave to set for 5-10 minutes before serving.

CRANBERRY, CHERRY AND BOURBON MINCE PIES

FOR THE MINCEMEAT
100g dried cranberries
100g dried cherries
115g vegetarian suet, shredded
1 Bramley apple, skin on, cored
   and cut into 1-cm cubes (about
   220g in total)
115g dark muscovado sugar
100g flaked almonds, roughly
   chopped
410g dried mixed fruit
Finely grated zest and juice of
   2 oranges
½ teaspoon ground ginger
½ teaspoon ground allspice
1 teaspoon ground mixed spice
½ teaspoon ground cinnamon
75ml Bourbon

FOR THE PASTRY
240g plain flour, plus extra for
   dusting
Pinch of salt
Finely grated zest of 1 orange
120g vegetable shortening,
   removed from the fridge
   10 minutes before using, diced
Iced water
Icing sugar, for dusting

About 3 sterilised jars
2 x 12-hole bun trays, lightly
   greased with dairy-free spread

Makes 24

Mince pies are the Marmite of Christmas foods – people either love them or hate them. I'm convinced the latter camp have been put off by sickly, soggy, shop-bought pies. These light little bakes – with a rich and juicy cranberry and cherry filling and short, flaky pastry – have converted many a refusenik.

Combine all the mincemeat ingredients, except for the Bourbon, in a large casserole and stir to combine. Put the lid on and leave overnight.

The next day, preheat the oven to 120°C/250°F/Gas Mark ½. Remove the lid, cover the top of the casserole with foil and bake for 3 hours. Leave to cool completely before stirring in the Bourbon. Spoon into the sterilised jars and leave for a minimum of 1-2 weeks before making your mince pies. Any mincemeat you don't use in the pies will keep for next Christmas if you store it in a cool, dark place.

To make the pies, sift the flour and salt into a bowl, lifting the sieve high above the bowl to get more air into the mixture. Stir in the orange zest, then add the diced vegetable shortening. Start by using two dinner knives to work the shortening into the flour until it is the texture of coarse breadcrumbs (you may find you need to use your hands after a while and, if so, make sure they are cold). Add enough iced water, a very little bit at a time and stirring it in with the knife, for the mixture to be just moist enough to bring together with your hands into a dough (you may not need it all). Gather it into a ball, wrap in clingfilm and chill for 30 minutes.

Place 2 flat baking trays in the oven and preheat to 220°C/425°F/Gas Mark 7. Take the chilled dough out of the fridge and roll it out on a lightly floured surface to a 1-2mm thickness (it should be very thin). Cut out 24 circles with a 7-cm round pastry cutter, and press into each hole of the bun trays. Pull the trimmings together into a ball and return briefly to the fridge while you fill each pastry case with 1 teaspoon mincemeat.

Roll the remaining dough out to 1-2mm thickness and use a small star cutter to cut out 24 star-shaped lids. Place these on top of the mincemeat; the points of the stars should touch the edge of the pie case. Transfer the bun trays to the preheated trays in the oven and bake for 10-12 minutes, until the tops are golden. Remove and leave to cool slightly on a wire rack before dusting with icing sugar.

JAMMY DOUGHNUTS

100ml almond milk

200g strong white bread flour

7-g sachet fast-action dried yeast

Good pinch of sea salt

20g caster sugar, plus extra
  to dust

1 egg

25g dairy-free sunflower spread,
  melted and cooled

Sunflower or vegetable oil,
  for deep-frying

Seedless jam – strawberry,
  raspberry or blueberry

Deep-fat fryer

Piping bag fitted with a
  thin nozzle

*Makes 8 medium or
10 smaller doughnuts*

The doughnut may have taken a recent turn in the spotlight (I'm looking at you, Cronut), but while all those headline-grabbing experiments and novelty flavours are fun, you can't beat a warm jammy doughnut dusted in sugar. They always remind me of standing against the wind on Brighton Pier, eating hot doughnuts from a paper bag while fending off seagulls.

Heat the almond milk in a small pan or in a microwave until lukewarm. Cover and leave to one side.

Sift the flour into a large mixing bowl. Mix in the yeast, salt and sugar, then make a well in the centre.

Whisk together the egg, warmed almond milk and melted spread, then pour into the well. Bring together into a large ball of dough. Transfer the dough to a lightly oiled work surface and knead for about 10 minutes, until smooth and bouncy (you can also do this with the dough hook attachment on a stand mixer if you don't fancy the upper-arm workout).

Place the dough in a lightly oiled, large bowl, cover with clingfilm and leave in a warm place (such as an airing cupboard) for about 1 hour, until doubled in size.

Divide the risen dough into 8-10 evenly sized pieces. Shape each piece into a ball, first by tucking all the edges underneath, then by rolling with your hands into a smooth ball. Place all the balls, well spaced apart, on a lined baking tray. Cover with a clean tea towel and leave to rise in a warm place for 45 minutes–1 hour – they should be nearly doubled in size.

Heat the oil in a deep fat fryer to 190°C and deep-fry the doughnuts in batches. Alternatively, heat the oil (carefully) to 190°C in a large, heavy-bottomed frying pan. The doughnuts are ready when they are golden brown all over. Remove to a plate lined with kitchen paper. Sprinkle caster sugar onto a separate plate and roll the hot doughnuts in it. Transfer to a wire rack and leave to cool for 10 minutes.

Use the tip of the piping bag nozzle or a skewer to make a hole in one side of each doughnut. Fill the piping bag two-thirds full with jam, then pipe a little into each hole. Serve warm.

HORCHATA WITH OATMEAL COOKIES

FOR THE HORCHATA
100g long-grain white rice
200g blanched almonds
1 cinnamon stick (Mexican if you
    can find it)
2 ½ tablespoons maple syrup
1 tablespoon vanilla extract
Pinch of sea salt
900ml cold, filtered water
A little ground cinnamon,
    to sprinkle (optional)

FOR THE COOKIES
75g raisins
115g dairy-free sunflower spread
140g soft brown sugar
70g plain flour
½ teaspoon baking powder
½ teaspoon ground cinnamon
Pinch of sea salt
1 medium egg
1 teaspoon vanilla extract
170g porridge oats

*Makes about 800ml horchata
and 10-12 medium cookies*

Here is the dairy-free answer to milk and cookies. Horchata originates from Valencia, where it's made with tiger nuts (*chufa*), which are tricky to find outside of Spain. You can drink it there in old-fashioned *horchaterías* lined with pretty tiles. Horchata travelled with the Spanish to Latin America and there are regional versions all over that continent. Mexican horchata is one of the best-known, and is usually made with rice and cinnamon. Almonds are often used too, and help make the milk really creamy. It makes the perfect partner to chewy oatmeal cookies, fragranced with cinnamon.

For the horchata, put the rice, almonds and cinnamon stick in a bowl. Cover with double the volume of cold tap water, cover and leave to soak for 8 hours or overnight.

For the cookies, soak the raisins in boiling water for 5 minutes. Drain then pat dry with kitchen paper. Grease and line 2 baking trays. Cream together the dairy-free spread and sugar, using a wooden spoon, until pale and fluffy. Sift the flour, baking powder, cinnamon and salt together in a separate bowl. Add the egg, vanilla and 1 tablespoon of the flour mixture to the sugar and dairy-free spread mixture and beat with an electric whisk, or paddle attachment of a stand mixer, until combined. Fold in the remaining flour mixture using a large metal spoon, then fold in the raisins and oats. Form the dough into a ball, wrap in clingfilm and chill in the fridge for 30 minutes. Meanwhile, preheat the oven to 180°C/350°F/Gas Mark 4.

Use an ice-cream scoop to scoop out cookie-sized balls of the chilled dough. Space these out well apart on the prepared baking trays (5-6 per tray) and flatten down slightly with a spoon. Bake for 10-12 minutes, or until golden around the edges but still soft-ish in the middle. Remove from the oven and leave to cool for 5 minutes, then transfer to a wire rack to cool completely.

Meanwhile, for the horchata, rinse and drain the rice, almonds and cinnamon. Chop the cinnamon stick into smaller pieces and add with the rice, almonds, maple syrup, vanilla and salt to a blender. Pour in the filtered water and blitz until the almonds, cinnamon and rice are broken up into very small pieces and you have a creamy liquid (this will take a few minutes). Place a fine-mesh sieve over a large bowl and line with a piece of muslin. Pour the horchata mixture into the sieve, using a wooden spoon to press down and push more liquid through. Add ice to hi-ball glasses and pour over the horchata. Serve with a little sprinkling of ground cinnamon on top, if desired, and the cookies.

SOUR CHERRY AND ALMOND FLAPJACKS

1 tablespoon coconut oil
150g dairy-free sunflower spread
75g golden syrup
150g soft brown sugar
300g porridge oats (look for
    gluten-free oats if you want
    to make this recipe g-f)
75g dried regular or sour
    cherries
40g toasted flaked almonds

26 x 19cm rectangular baking tin,
    greased and lined

Makes 12

Banish the butter and make traditional flapjacks with dairy-free spread to bind, and a little coconut oil for taste – its subtle flavour masks the spread and pairs well with the tang of dried cherries (sweet or sour) and toasty almonds.

Preheat the oven to 190°C/375°F/Gas Mark 5.

Melt the coconut oil and dairy-free spread with the syrup and sugar over a low heat, stirring with a wooden spoon until all the ingredients have melted and are combined. Stir until a dark golden colour, then stir in the oats, dried cherries and flaked almonds.

Spread the mixture into the prepared tin. Cover any cherries poking out of the top with oats to stop them burning in the oven, and press the top down firmly with the back of a wooden spoon.

Bake for 25-30 minutes until starting to turn golden.

Remove from the oven and leave to cool in the tin for 5 minutes before scoring 12 squares with a sharp knife. Leave to cool completely in the tin before cutting into squares. Store in an airtight container for a few days.

PHILIPPA'S LEMON MERINGUE CAKE

250g dairy-free sunflower spread
250g caster sugar
4 medium eggs
200g self-raising flour, sifted
Grated zest of 2 lemons (long
    strands are preferable) and
    1 tablespoon juice
2 tablespoons soya or almond
    milk
75g ground almonds
1 ½ teaspoons baking powder

FOR THE FILLING AND TOP
4 egg whites
300g caster sugar
1 quantity lemon curd
    (see page 143)

20-cm round, deep cake tin
    greased and lined with
    greaseproof paper
piping bag, fitted with a plain
    nozzle
kitchen blowtorch

Serves 8-10

My friend Philippa is an amazing baker and creates beautiful, towering wedding cakes and birthday confections in her spare time. On my hen do, my friends surprised me with a dairy-free afternoon tea, and Philippa's three-tiered lemon cake with toasted peaks of meringue was the spectacular centrepiece...

Preheat the oven to 180°C/350°F/Gas Mark 4.

Using an electric whisk, or the paddle attachment of a stand mixer, beat the dairy-free spread with the sugar until pale and fluffy. Whisk in the eggs, one at a time, alternating each with 1 tablespoon of the flour and whisking to combine. Mix in the lemon zest, juice and soya or almond milk. Fold in the remaining sifted flour, the ground almonds and baking powder using a large metal spoon.

Spoon the batter into the prepared tin and bake for 1 hour-1 hour 15 minutes. To test whether the cake is cooked all the way through, pop a wooden stick (kebab stick is perfect!) into the centre and push all the way down. If it is sticky when removed then the cake will need more time, and if a few crumbs stick to the sides then the cake is ready to come out.

Leave the cake in the tin for 5 minutes, then remove from the tin and transfer to a wire rack to cool completely. When the cake is completely cool, cut horizontally into equal thirds using a bread knife (rounded tip is best) or a cake leveller.

For the filling, put the egg whites and sugar in a bowl set over a pan of simmering water and whisk on a high speed, using a hand-held electric whisk, for 5-10 minutes until the mixture is thick and glossy with stiff peaks.

Place one layer of the sponge on a plate or cake stand, spread with lemon curd, then a layer of the soft meringue. Place another layer of sponge on top, and repeat.

Add the final layer of sponge and, using a piping bag, pipe small whirls of the soft meringue over the top until it is fully covered. Alternatively, you can use a palette knife to spread a layer of meringue of the top and create little peaks for texture. Using a kitchen blowtorch, lightly flame the peaks so that they colour on top.

PASSIONFRUIT FRIANDS

5 egg whites
225g icing sugar, plus extra
    for dusting (optional)
125g ground almonds
75g plain flour, sifted
180g dairy-free sunflower spread,
    melted and cooled
½ teaspoon vanilla extract
Pulp of 2 passionfruits

12-hole friand or cupcake tin,
    well greased with dairy-free
    spread

Makes 12

Walk into any good café in Sydney or Melbourne and you'll see a rack of friands on the counter. These airy cakes get their name from the French word *friandise* – meaning dainty or confection. The delicate vanilla sponge is studded with sharp passionfruit, a combination that proves irresistible to everyone who crosses its path.

Preheat the oven to 200°C/400°F/Gas Mark 6.

Whisk the egg whites in a very clean bowl, using an electric mixer, for a couple of minutes until white and frothy.

Sift the icing sugar onto the egg whites. Add the ground almonds, sifted flour, melted spread, vanilla and passionfruit pulp. Use a large metal spoon to gently fold everything into the egg whites, trying not to knock out too much air.

Divide the mixture equally between the holes of the greased friand tray. Bake for 20 minutes in the preheated oven, or until golden around the edges and lightly golden on top, and a small skewer or cocktail stick inserted into the centre of one comes out clean.

Leave to cool for 5 minutes in the tin, before turning out onto a wire rack to cool further (use a dinner knife to help get them out of the tin - go around the edges and then lift out with the knife). Dust with a little icing sugar if you like.

LEMON AND ROSEMARY OLIVE OIL CAKE

Finely grated zest of 3 lemons
4–5 teaspoons fresh rosemary
   needles, very finely chopped
   (depending on how
   pronounced you want the
   rosemary flavour to be)
225g caster sugar
245ml olive oil
4 eggs
225g self-raising flour, sifted
Pinch of salt

FOR THE DRIZZLE TOPPING
Juice of 1 ½ lemons
50ml water
80g caster sugar
Zest of ½ lemon (try to get
   long strands using a zester),
   to garnish

900g/2lb loaf tin, greased
   and lined

Serves 8–10

This is a cross between a classic British lemon drizzle cake and a sultry, Mediterranean olive oil cake. The fresh lemon zest and hint of rosemary make me think of shaded Italian squares, hiking in Cypriot pine forests and late nights fuelled by limoncello - even when eating a slice on a rainy day, accompanied by nothing stronger than a big mug of tea.

Preheat the oven to 180°C/350°F/Gas Mark 4.

Rub half of the lemon zest and the rosemary into the sugar with your fingers. Beat the olive oil and sugar together with an electric whisk or with the paddle attachment of a stand mixer for a couple of minutes.

Add the eggs one at a time, alternating with a tablespoon of the flour, and whisk to combine. Fold in the remaining flour using a large metal spoon, until just combined. Fold in the other half of the lemon zest, and the salt.

Pour the mixture into the loaf tin and bake for 45-50 minutes, or until the top is golden and a skewer or toothpick inserted into the middle comes out clean.

Remove the cake from the oven and leave to cool for 5-10 minutes in the tin before turning out onto a wire rack with a sheet of kitchen foil spread underneath it. Prick small holes all over the top of the cake with a fork or a skewer.

While the cake is cooling, make the drizzle topping. Heat the lemon juice in a saucepan along with the water. Add the sugar and bring to the boil, stirring occasionally. Boil for 3 minutes or until all the sugar has dissolved and the mixture has a runny, syrupy consistency, then remove from the heat and leave to cool slightly.

While the cake is still warm, pour half of the syrup all over the top of the cake and allow it to sink in before pouring over the other half, allowing some to drip down the sides. Garnish with lemon zest.

STRAWBERRY AND ELDERFLOWER MILLEFEUILLE

250ml coconut cream
1 tablespoon icing sugar,
    plus extra for sprinkling
500g ready-made puff pastry
    (NOT the all-butter kind)
1½ tablespoons elderflower
    cordial
220g ripe strawberries, trimmed
    and thinly sliced (about 4mm),
    plus extra, whole, to serve
Fresh elderflower heads,
    to decorate (optional)

Makes 6

Millefeuille is a classic French confection – tiers of pastry and cream which translates as 'a thousand leaves'. Meanwhile, the combination of strawberries and heady elderflowers is as English as Wimbledon and country garden parties. Think of this as an Anglo-French alliance in pastry form.

Chill the coconut cream in its carton or can in the fridge for at least 4–6 hours and preferably overnight.

Preheat the oven to 200°C/400°F/Gas Mark 6 and place a large baking tray in to heat. Grease and line a second large baking tray.

Flour the work surface with the icing sugar. Roll out the pastry into a large rectangle, about 30 x 26cm and 2–3mm thick. Trim the edges, using a ruler to ensure a straight line.

Drape the pastry over a rolling pin and carefully unfurl onto the lined baking tray. Prick the pastry all over lightly with a fork and sprinkle with a little more icing sugar. Place the preheated baking tray on top to weigh down the pastry, then place a heavy casserole on top of this to really weigh it down. Transfer to the oven and bake for 25 minutes or until the pastry is golden. Remove from the oven and leave to cool.

When the pastry is cool, and with a long side facing you, use a sharp knife and a ruler to cut the pastry into 3 evenly sized rows across and 6 evenly sized rows down, to give 18 rectangles of the same size.

To make elderflower cream, take the coconut cream out of the fridge and pour away any watery liquid. Whisk with the elderflower cordial using a hand-held electric whisk until thick and fluffy, for 3–4 minutes.

To assemble a millefeuille, spoon some elderflower cream onto a pastry rectangle. Lay strawberry slices flat on top, then top with another pastry rectangle. Repeat, then top with a final pastry rectangle, so that each millefeuille has 3 layers of pastry. Use a small, fine-mesh sieve to dust the top with icing sugar. Smooth the edges using the edge of a palette knife so the cream and pastry form neat sides. Repeat to make 6 millefeuille in total. Serve with extra strawberries on the side and decorate with fresh elderflowers, if you can find them.

NEAPOLITAN ICED BUNS

200ml almond milk
500g strong white bread flour,
   plus extra for dusting
7-g sachet fast-action dried yeast
Generous pinch of sea salt
50g caster sugar
2 eggs
85ml water

FOR THE ICING
300g icing sugar
1-2 tablespoons boiling water
½ teaspoon vanilla extract
½ tablespoon cocoa powder
½ teaspoon strawberry
   flavouring
¼ teaspoon pink food colouring

Makes 12

While my childhood snacking policy could be summarised as Chocolate First, there were other sweet treats that caught my fancy. Iced buns – those long, soft subs topped with a thick slick of icing were one. Neapolitan ice cream, evenly portioned into a flag of strawberry, vanilla and (of course) chocolate ice cream, was another. Iced buns have a bread roll base, so are naturally dairy-free; Neapolitan ice cream is obviously not. So I've combined these two retro favourites into one. Presenting...Neapolitan iced buns.

Heat the almond milk in a small pan or in the microwave until lukewarm. Cover and leave to one side.

Sift the flour into a large bowl. Mix in the yeast, salt and sugar then make a well in the centre. Whisk together the eggs, warmed almond milk and water, then pour into the well. Bring together into a ball of dough, knead lightly for a couple of minutes in the bowl, then transfer to a floured surface and knead for 10 minutes, until smooth and bouncy. (You can also use the dough hook attachment on a stand mixer, if you don't fancy the upper-arm workout.) Transfer the dough to a lightly oiled bowl. Cover with clingfilm and leave in a warm place (such as an airing cupboard) for about 1 hour, until doubled in size.

Divide the dough into 12 evenly sized pieces. Shape each piece into a ball, first by tucking all the edges underneath, then by rolling with your hands into a smooth ball. Roll out each ball into a sausage shape, or 'finger', about 8cm long. Line a large baking tray with baking parchment, then arrange the 12 dough fingers, evenly spaced, on the tray. Cover with a tea towel and leave to rise in a warm place for 45 minutes – they should be nearly doubled in size. Meanwhile, preheat the oven to 200°C/400°F/Gas Mark 6.

Bake the risen buns for 12 minutes or until golden, then transfer to a wire rack to cool completely. Once cool, make the icing. Sift the icing sugar into a bowl and whisk in enough boiling water to make a smooth, stiff paste. Divide into 3 bowls. Whisk vanilla extract into one, and cocoa powder into another (plus a little extra water if needed to loosen just slightly). Whisk the strawberry flavouring into the third bowl of icing. Check to taste before adding the pink food colouring a drop at a time, just until you get a pastel pink shade.

Dip 4 of the buns into the vanilla icing, 4 into the chocolate icing, and 4 into the strawberry icing. Leave the icing to set then eat.

FAIRY CAKES

100g dairy-free sunflower spread
100g golden caster sugar
2 large eggs
100g self-raising flour
1 teaspoon vanilla extract

FOR THE ICING
150g icing sugar
1 tablespoon boiling water
Hundreds and thousands,
    sprinkles or sugar stars to
    decorate (always check the
    label to make sure they
    don't contain milk powder)

12-hole bun tray, lined with fairy
    cake cases

Makes 12

Fairy cakes are the cupcake's smaller, less showy sister. These dainty, old-fashioned bakes are topped with a pond of glacé icing and a smattering of sprinkles. My dairy-free version is the perfect cake recipe for children: they're easy to make together (as long as you don't mind icing sugar EVERYWHERE), and you can take them along to a birthday party or fête and make another dairy-free kid's day.

Preheat the oven to 180°C/350°F/Gas Mark 4.

Cream the sunflower spread and sugar together in a large bowl using an electric whisk or the paddle attachment on a stand mixer until the mixture is very pale and fluffy and all the sugar is incorporated, about 2-3 minutes.

Add one of the eggs and half the flour to the mixture and beat again until incorporated. Add the remaining egg, the remaining flour and the vanilla, and beat again.

Divide the mixture evenly between the cases and bake for 20-25 minutes in the preheated oven until the tops are golden and a toothpick inserted into the centre of one of the cakes comes out clean. Turn the cakes out onto a wire rack and leave to cool.

To make the glacé icing, sift the icing sugar into a bowl and add the boiling water. Mix to a thick, smooth paste, then spread over each cake using the back of a teaspoon. Sprinkle each cake immediately with decorations and leave the icing to set before eating.

RAINY-DAY CARROT CAKES

100g sultanas
125ml sunflower, vegetable or
    rapeseed oil
180g soft brown sugar
100g self-raising flour
100g wholegrain spelt flour
1 teaspoon baking powder
½ teaspoon bicarbonate of soda
Pinch of salt
2 teaspoons ground cinnamon
1 teaspoon ground mixed spice
50g walnuts, chopped into very
    small pieces
2 eggs
200g carrots, peeled and
    coarsely grated

FOR THE FROSTING
1½ lemons (for zesting) and
    2 teaspoons juice
225g vegan cream cheese such
    as Tofutti
150g icing sugar, sifted
Pinch of salt

26 x 19cm rectangular cake tin,
    greased and lined

*Makes 12 large squares or
24 small ones*

It's raining, it's pouring and the sky is the colour of a wet seal – what you need is a square of carrot cake topped with zesty lemon frosting. Hopefully you'll have everything you need to make the cake in your cupboards already, though sourcing the vegan cream cheese might take a little forethought (it's widely available from health food shops).

Soak the sultanas in a little boiling water for 5 minutes to plump them up. Drain and pat dry with kitchen paper. Preheat the oven to 170°C/325°F/Gas Mark 3.

Beat the oil and sugar together using an electric whisk or with the paddle attachment of a stand mixer, for a couple of minutes.

Sift the flours, baking powder, bicarbonate of soda, salt, cinnamon and mixed spice into a large bowl. Use 1–2 tablespoons of this flour mixture to lightly coat the walnut pieces and sultanas, in a separate bowl (to help stop them sinking in the cake).

Add the eggs to the oil and sugar mixture, one at a time, alternating each with a tablespoon of the flour mixture and whisking to combine.

Fold in the remaining flour mixture using a large metal spoon, just until combined. Fold in the carrots and then the walnuts and sultanas.

Spoon the mixture into the prepared cake tin and smooth the top. Bake for 35 minutes, or until a skewer or cocktail stick inserted into the middle comes out clean. Leave to cool in the tin for 5 minutes, then transfer to a wire rack to cool completely.

For the frosting, finely grate 1 tablespoon of lemon zest. Whisk the vegan cream cheese, icing sugar, the lemon zest and juice together, using an electric whisk or the paddle attachment of a stand mixer, for 3–4 minutes until fluffy and any clumps of icing sugar have disappeared. Refrigerate until the cake is completely cool.

Once the cake is completely cool, spread the frosting on the top of the cake, right to the edges, smoothing the top and edges with a palette knife. Cut into squares. Use a lemon zester to zest long strands of the remaining lemon zest and use to garnish each square.

RASPBERRY AND DARK CHOCOLATE MUFFINS

100g dairy-free sunflower spread
125g wholegrain spelt flour
125g plain flour
1 teaspoon bicarbonate of soda
2 teaspoons baking powder
100g golden caster sugar
130g dark chocolate, chopped
   into very small chunks
150g raspberries
2 eggs, beaten
150ml vegetable oil
1 tablespoon granulated sugar,
   to sprinkle

12-hole muffin tray, lined with
   muffin cases

Makes 12

Shop-bought muffins aren't a patch on homemade, especially the 'free-from' ones with all those unpronounceable ingredients. These muffins are a doddle to make, and crammed with sharp raspberries and chunks of dark chocolate.

Melt the dairy-free spread in a small saucepan over a low heat and leave to one side to cool completely. Preheat the oven to 200°C/400°F/Gas Mark 6.

Sift both flours into a large mixing bowl. Add the bicarbonate of soda and baking powder and fold together gently using a large metal spoon. Gently fold in the sugar, chocolate chunks and raspberries, still using the large metal spoon.

Add the beaten eggs, oil, and the cooled, melted spread. Stir just until all the ingredients are combined – don't overmix. The raspberries will break up as you fold.

Fill each muffin case almost to the top (using an ice-cream scoop helps get the same amount into each case), and sprinkle the tops with a little granulated sugar. Bake for 15–20 minutes or until golden.

Cool on a wire rack. The muffins taste best when still slightly warm, while the chocolate is still melted and cosy inside.

DARK CHOCOLATE
AND PEAR BANANA BREAD

3 medium, or 2 large, very ripe
    bananas (about 400g)
150g block baking margarine,
    such as Stork (NOT the
    spreadable kind), at room
    temperature
150g soft brown sugar
150g plain flour
150g wholegrain spelt flour
2 teaspoons baking powder
½ teaspoon bicarbonate of soda
3 teaspoons ground ginger
Pinch of salt
50g dried pears, cut into
    5-mm cubes
2 medium eggs
100ml rapeseed or vegetable oil
75g dark chocolate, chopped into
    very small pieces

900g/2lb loaf tin, greased and
    lined

Makes 1 loaf

A throw-together banana bread fragranced with a little ginger and
with nuggets of melted dark chocolate and juicy pear hidden inside...

Preheat the oven to 180°C/350°F/Gas Mark 4.

Mash the bananas with a fork. In a separate bowl, cream the baking
margarine and sugar together with an electric whisk or with the
paddle attachment of a stand mixer until pale and fluffy. Stir in the
bananas with a large metal spoon.

Sift the flours, baking powder, bicarbonate of soda, ground ginger
and salt together in another bowl. Toss the diced pear pieces in
2 tablespoons of the flour mixture and set aside.

Add the eggs to the creamed sugar and banana mixture one at a time,
alternating with a tablespoon of the flour mixture and beating after
each addition. Fold in the rest of the flour mixture with a large metal
spoon, until just combined. Next, stir in the oil until just combined,
then fold in the dark chocolate and pear pieces.

Spoon the mixture into the loaf tin and smooth the top. Bake in the
preheated oven for 45–50 minutes or until the top is dark golden and
a skewer or cocktail stick inserted into the middle comes out clean.

Leave to cool in the tin for 5 minutes before turning out onto a wire
rack. Leave to cool completely before slicing.

GINGERBREAD GENTLEMEN

300g plain flour, plus extra for
   dusting
3 teaspoons ground ginger
½ teaspoon ground mixed spice
1 teaspoon ground cinnamon
Pinch of salt
1 teaspoon bicarbonate of soda
130g block baking margarine,
   such as Stork (NOT the
   spreadable kind), at room
   temperature, cut
   into small cubes
100g soft brown sugar
1 egg
3 tablespoons golden syrup

TO DECORATE
Black icing writing pen
White icing writing pen

Gingerbread man cutter

*Makes around 16-20 depending
on the size of your cutter*

Meet the gingerbread gentlemen: aristocrats with jaunty iced bow-ties
and monocles. These Bertie Wooster biscuits make for a thoughtful
gift, packaged in clear cellophane bags and tied with a ribbon. Best
accompanied with a large pot of Earl Grey tea... and a butler.

Sift the flour, spices, salt and bicarbonate of soda together in a
large bowl.

Beat the margarine and sugar together with an electric whisk or the
paddle attachment of a stand mixer until pale and fluffy. Add the egg
and 1 tablespoon of the flour mixture and whisk briefly to combine,
then whisk in the syrup. Fold in the remaining flour using a large
metal spoon to combine, and bring it together with your hands into a
ball of dough. Wrap in clingfilm and chill in the fridge for 30 minutes.
Meanwhile, preheat the oven to 170°C/325°F/Gas Mark 3. Grease and
line 2 baking trays.

Lightly flour a work surface and roll the dough out with a rolling pin to
a thickness of about 4mm. Cut out biscuits using a gingerbread-man
cutter and space them out on the prepared baking trays - 8-10 on
each tray.

Bake for 15 minutes or until golden. Leave the biscuits to cool for
5 minutes on the baking trays, then transfer to a wire rack to cool
completely.

Once cool, use the white icing pen to draw on details such as a shirt
collar, buttons, mouth and eyes. Use the black icing writing pen to
draw irises in the eyes, a monocle around one eye and a bow-tie
(use the white icing pen if you want your gentlemen to be sporting
white tie).

DAIRY-FREE DIRECTORY

I've tried, wherever possible, to use ingredients which are easy to track down in your local supermarket or health food shop. Here's where to track down some harder-to-find items, along with brand recommendations and websites.

ALMOND MILK

Almond milk is now widely available and stocked in all the UK supermarkets. You'll increasingly find it available in cafés, too. There are lots of brands on the market. I think unsweetened tastes fresher and more pleasant, and is always my preferred choice for cooking. Look for brands made with non-GM ingredients. Some are also fortified with vitamins and additional calcium. I like Almond Breeze (made by Blue Diamond), and Rude Health's Almond Drink. (Please note the Rude Health drink contains rice as well so is not suitable for under 5s.)

www.bluediamondalmonds.co.uk
www.rudehealth.com

BASIL TOFU

Try Taifun basil tofu, which is available from Waitrose, Ocado and some health food shops.

www.taifun-tofu.de/en

CACAO NIBS

Most health food shops will now stock cacao nibs. Brace yourself for the price as they are not cheap (around £8 for a 250g bag), but a little will go a very long way. Booja-Booja Cacao Nibs can be found in health food stores across the UK, as well as some branches of Waitrose and Whole Foods. Infinity Foods Organic Cacao Nibs is a good brand to look for in health shops and can also be found online.

www.boojabooja.com
www.infinityfoodswholesale.co.uk
(has a stockist locator on its website)

COCOA POWDER

Cocoa powder is available in all major supermarkets, but check the label to make sure it doesn't contain milk in the ingredients. I like Green & Blacks Organic Cocoa which should be fine if you have a lactose intolerance, as it doesn't contain any dairy ingredients. However, like most cocoas it does have a 'may contain milk' disclaimer because of the factory where it is produced. Cocoa powder produced in a milk-free factory can be tricky to find. If you have a milk-protein allergy, try Plamil's dairy-free and organic Chocolate Flakes, which can be used to make hot chocolate and in cooking.

www.greenandblacks.co.uk
www.plamilfoods.co.uk

COCONUT CREAM AND MILK

There are dozens of brands of coconut milk in the UK, and I've tried most of them! For whipped coconut cream I get the best results from chilling a carton of Blue Dragon Coconut Cream. The milk is pretty creamy too, as is Sainsbury's own-brand coconut milk. Please note that it's coconut cream you're after, rather than creamed coconut (which is sold in solid blocks).

www.bluedragon.co.uk
www.sainsburys.co.uk

COCONUT OIL

You should now find coconut oil stocked in the same supermarket aisle as olive and sunflower. There are several decent options on the market including Tiana Extra Virgin Coconut Oil and Lucy Bee Organic Coconut Oil. Both are Fairtrade, extra virgin and organic.

www.tiana-coconut.com
http://www.lucybee.co

COCONUT YOGURT

Co Yo is a great coconut yogurt brand available in several UK supermarkets and from Ocado. It makes both small and medium tubs of its plain yogurt; the latter are most useful for cooking. I also like The Coconut Collaborative.

www.coyo.co.uk
www.coconutco.co.uk

DAIRY-FREE SUNFLOWER SPREAD

I use Pure Sunflower Spread, which is available from most major supermarkets.

www.puredairyfree.co.uk

DARK CHOCOLATE

70% cocoa-solids dark chocolate is widely available. As with cocoa powder, dark chocolate sometimes comes with a 'may contain milk traces' warning if it was made in a factory that also handles milk products. If you have a milk protein allergy, try Plamil instead.

www.greenandblacks.co.uk
www.plamilfoods.co.uk

OAT CREAM

Oatly produces cartons of oat cream which are stocked in some branches of Waitrose and Holland & Barrett, as well as independent health shops. (It's called 'Organic Creamy Oat' and has a similar consistency to single cream.)

www.oatly.com

PANKO

Increasingly available in supermarkets, from Japanese and Asian grocery stores and from online retailers like Ocado. Most brands I've tried, including Blue Dragon and Saitaku, have been pretty good.

www.bluedragon.co.uk
www.saitaku-food.com/en

SOYA YOGURT

I use plain Alpro Soya Yogurt.

www.alpro.com/

VANILLA POWDER

A little pot of vanilla powder goes a long way, helps make those dairy-free bakes taste delicious, and takes away the faff of scraping vanilla seeds from a pod. Ndali Vanilla Powder is organic and Fairtrade. You can currently find it in Waitrose and online from Ocado.

www.ndali.net

VEGAN CREAM CHEESE

Tofutti is the brand to look for. Find it at Holland & Barrett and in independent health food shops. You can also source it online from the excellent Goodness Direct.

www.goodnessdirect.co.uk

Stockist details correct at time of going to press.

For more help, recommendations and tips on going dairy free, visit my website:
dairyfreedelicious.com

ACKNOWLEDGEMENTS

Although this book has my name on the cover, it wouldn't have happened without the support and creativity of some very talented and generous people.

Firstly, thanks to everyone at Quadrille. Thanks for making this book look even better than I'd dared hope. Huge thanks to Jane O'Shea for believing in the idea and understanding that it should be joyful and beautiful, not preachy or dull. I'm indebted to Céline Hughes for her advice and thoughtful editing. Thanks to Helen Lewis and Katherine Keeble for the gorgeous design. And thanks to publicity whizz, Ed Griffiths, and the sales team.

To my agent Tim Bates - thanks for believing in me and in this project, and for all those Notes coffees.

Laura Edwards - thanks for your gorgeous photos. You are such a talent and I'm so glad you shot this book. Tabitha Hawkins - no-one in the world does props better than you.

Thanks to the lovely Emily Jonzen for your super styling and perfection with a citrus zester, ably assisted by Poppy Campbell and Camilla Baynham. Ladies, you all made the shoot such a blast.

Thanks to the editors who encourage me and commission me - particularly Susan Smillie at *The Guardian* and Sarah Randell and Helena Lang at *Sainsbury's Magazine*. Plus William Sitwell, to whom I owe a huge amount.

Thanks to Sarah Tye at Gemma Bell PR and Carl Brown at Dishoom for the Bombay Colada recipe.

Huge love to my family for their help in testing (and enthusiastically eating) all those bakes: Jo and Trevor Salter, Ed, Jess and Finley Salter. Sorry if your freezers are still full of cake. Plus, a big thanks to my crack recipe testers and supportive friends, Ellie Porter, Vanessa Brooks and Elaine Brooks. Philippa Tuck is a baking queen - thank you Flips for your amazing lemon meringue sponge recipe. Thanks to Lucia Rae, Adrienne Pitts and Sukhpal Sahota for encouragement and for that Sunday-afternoon shoot when this book was still very much an idea.

Finally, thanks to Jon Yeomans, my no.1 cheer-person, washer-up-in-chief, proof reader and consumer of countless recipe tests. I couldn't have done it without you.